Judy Ridgway is a full-time cookery writer and consultant with over twenty cookery books to her name, covering topics as diverse as vegetarian gourmet cooking, home preserving, barbecues, fish cookery, toasted sandwiches and children's books. She also does some broadcasting and consultancy work and runs a small catering business in the London area called London Cooks.

Also available from Century Arrow

Wheat & Gluten Free

COOKERY

OVER 100 RECIPES FOR ALLERGY SUFFERERS

JUDY RIDGWAY

CENTURY ARROW

LONDON   MELBOURNE   AUCKLAND   JOHANNESBURG

A Century Arrow Book
Published by Arrow Books Ltd
62–65 Chandos Place, London WC2N 4NW

An imprint of Century Hutchinson Ltd

London Melbourne Sydney Auckland Johannesburg
and agencies throughout the world
First published 1986
Copyright © by Judy Ridgway 1986
Illustrations by Kate Simunek

ISBN 0 09 946650 3

Photoset by Rowland Phototypesetting Ltd, Bury St Edmunds
Printed in Great Britain in 1986 by
The Guernsey Press Ltd, Guernsey, Channel Islands

Contents

Foreword by Dr Vicky Rippere   vi
Introduction   1
1   Bread   5
2   Breakfast   20
3   Soup   32
4   Soufflés and Savoury Dishes   41
5   Snacks and Canapés   56
6   Stuffings and Coatings   66
7   Sauces   77
8   Pies, Tarts and Flans   81
9   Puddings   95
10   Cakes, Buns and Biscuits   108
Appendix   128
Index   130

Foreword

Gluten sensitivity is an as yet incompletely understood cause of several serious medical conditions. The most familiar of these is coeliac disease, in which gluten—a protein contained in wheat, rye, barley, and oats—causes damage to the tiny fingerlike projections known as villi which line the small intestine and serve to create a large surface through which absorption of the nutrients available from the digestion of food may take place. In coeliac disease gluten causes these villi to atrophy, which results in malabsorption of nutrients accompanied by diarrhoea, abdominal pain, offensive stools, and wasting or failure to thrive. Coeliac disease is a serious affliction which, before the discovery of the role of gluten in its causation and the use of gluten-free diets as treatment, caused death in about a third of the children in which it occurred. Even quite recently deaths in adult cases continue to be reported.

Another important gluten-related condition is dermatitis herpetiformis, a blistering disorder of the skin, which in many cases is associated with the same sort of villous atrophy as is found in coeliac disease. In this condition, response to a gluten-free diet is reported to be less predictable, but many sufferers are nonetheless found to benefit.

In addition to these relatively well-established results of gluten sensitivity, evidence is also being produced to show that some, though not all, sufferers from schizophrenia, multiple sclerosis, infantile autism, rheumatoid arthritis, and regional enteritis (inflammation of the large intestine) show adverse reactions to this constituent of their daily bread.

Besides these serious diseases, there are also a few less dire conditions which, in some people, at least, improve when gluten is removed from the diet and recur when it is reintroduced. Headaches and mouth ulcers sometimes come into this category and no doubt others would be found if the possibility of causation by gluten was more readily suspected. Of course, not everyone who has these symptoms is showing adverse reactions to gluten, but in cases where all else has failed, the possibility is always worth considering.

Finally, it has even been found that normal healthy people can start to show structural changes characteristic of coeliac disease in the small intestine and apparently normal relatives of coeliacs can develop diarrhoea as well if they increase their consumption of gluten substantially. It is coming to be suspected that a high consumption of gluten may be the trigger for the development of coeliac disease in many adult cases.

Thus the number of people who might benefit from adopting a gluten-free diet is much greater than might initially appear. But, having been advised by a doctor or decided on one's own initiative to eliminate all gluten from one's intake, where does one start? Probably the most common cause of failure to benefit from a gluten-free diet is the inability to exclude every last trace of gluten. With a substance as ubiquitous in the typical modern diet as gluten, a guidebook is obviously needed.

One of the things a guidebook must do if it is to be effective is to explain what gluten is and where it is found. Another, equally important, is to make clear where it is *not* found and how to prepare the foods that are safe to eat in ways that are varied, interesting, nourishing, and straight-forward, so that sufferers from gluten sensitivity can enjoy a standard of eating that is as good or even better than that of people who are able to eat an unrestricted diet. Judy Ridg-way's book meets all of these requirements and goes beyond them. I would be happy to recommend it, but it really needs no recommendation. With its great range of interesting, nourishing and practical recipes, the book speaks for itself.

Dr Vicky Rippere, PhD, MPhil

Introduction

What is gluten and where does it occur?

Gluten is a protein which occurs in certain cereals. It is, in fact, the substance that gives both binding quality and elasticity to flours made from these cereals.

Wheat has a particularly good concentration of gluten in its make up. This can be demonstrated by taking a spoonful of wheatflour and mixing it with a little water. The result will be a firmly bound paste which can be pulled into quite long lengths.

Rye, barley and oats also contain gluten but to a lesser degree than wheat, and bread and cakes made with these flours do not have quite the rising quality of those made with conventional flour.

Wheatflour is one of the most widely used products. It is wheatflour which is bought when a recipe specifies flour and this is true for plain, self-raising, strong, sponge, wheatmeal or wholemeal flour.

The fact that gluten is present in these flours of course means that anything made with them is forbidden to anyone who cannot eat gluten. This obviously takes in bread, cakes, buns, biscuits, pastries and steamed puddings. But it can also present difficulties with sauces, stuffings, soups and savoury dishes such as soufflés, batters and pancakes and pasta dishes.

Gluten-free foods

There are plenty of gluten-free foods and these take in all fruit and vegetables, meat and fish and dairy produce. They also include nuts, pulses, seeds, oils and margarine.

Luckily, there are also quite a few cereals which are gluten-free and these include rice, millet, corn (Indian or sweetcorn) and buckwheat.

All of these cereals are available in forms which can be used in baking and to substitute for wheatflour in the sort of savoury dishes listed previously. Available forms include:

RICE
Brown rice and polished rice in short, medium and long-grain versions: use in stuffings and puddings and as an accompaniment to other foods.

Flaked rice: use in breakfast cereal mixes such as porridge or muesli, in puddings and as the base for soufflé mixtures and savoury dishes. Grind and use as a coating for frying or baking.
Ground rice: use in bread, cakes and biscuits and in puddings.
Rice flour: use with other flours in bread, cakes, biscuits, pastry and almost all savoury applications.
Rice noodles: use as pasta or Chinese egg noodles.

MILLET
Whole millet: use as long-grain rice.
Flaked millet: use in breakfast cereal mixes such as porridge or muesli. In puddings and as the base for soufflé mixtures, stuffings and other savoury dishes. Grind and use as a coating for frying or baking or use for bread pancakes.

CORN
Whole sweetcorn kernels: use as a vegetable or grind and use in batter mixture.

Yellow cornmeal, coarse, medium and fine: use in bread, cakes and biscuits. Also in pastry and almost all savoury applications.
Maizemeal or maize flour: this includes the whole of the grain. Use as cornflour.
Cornflour: check that the product is gluten-free and use on its own or mixed with other flours in all applications.

BUCKWHEAT
Buckwheat noodles: check that the product is gluten-free and use as pasta.
Buckwheat flour: use with other flours in bread and pan-cakes.

There are also a variety of other flours which can be used in gluten-free cooking. They tend to be a little more difficult to find.

BEAN OR SPLIT GREEN PEA BASE
Flour made from these pulses can be bought at both Indian and Chinese grocers. In Indian shops they may have various names including Channa, Baisan or Grain flour. You may also find roasted chickpea flour or Moong and Urad dal which are made from other beans.

One of the most useful bean-based flours is soya flour. It is available from most health food shops. Use with other flours in all kinds of bread, cakes, biscuits and puddings.

POTATO BASE

Potato flour can be used with other flours in bread, cakes, biscuits, pastries and almost all savoury applications. Instant dried mashed potato powder can also be used in sauces or to thicken casseroles.

MIXED BASES

There are a variety of special gluten-free flours and mixes on the market. They are available from health food shops. Some have a mixed base and others simply have the gluten removed from ordinary flour. If you have a wheat allergy you will need to check which is which. For details of some of these flours, see the Appendix.

Note: All dishes are for four people unless otherwise specified.

I

Bread

Bread is eaten at almost every meal in the Western diet and of course it is made almost exclusively from wheat. If you cannot eat wheat you have a major problem on your hands. However, there *are* ways round it.

First of all there are a number of ready-made gluten-free breads on the market, but you will have to make a trek to the nearest specialist health food shop to find them. Most of them are specially packed and will keep for a few weeks if unopened.

The different brands vary in taste and texture. I found that while they cut quite well and have a reasonable texture the flavour is a little strange. This flavour does improve on toasting.

If you have the time, homemade bread is probably preferable. To make loaves reasonably similar to the bread you have been used to you may have to buy some of the specialist gluten-free flour mixes. These are expensive but the loaves do work out cheaper than ready-made ones.

On the other hand I have worked out some recipes which use relatively cheap ingredients and which produce loaves which are almost indistinguishable from real bread. Buckwheat Loaf (page 9) is one of these. It is a little grey in colour but has a flavour and texture which compares very favourably with wholemeal bread.

The texture and flavour of breads made with the specialist flours are also quite good—though I did find that, contrary to the manufacturer's notes, a short rising period of 5 minutes or so did improve the texture. The loaves will slice thinly and toast well. The flavour is acceptable and certainly better than the bought loaves I tried. If you flavour your loaves with sesame seeds, honey or dried fruit the result is indistinguishable from other homemade breads.

American cornbread makes a very good replacement for bread eaten with the hot meal of the day. However, it should be eaten fresh and hot. It won't really keep. Other ideas include savoury Drop Scones, Potato Cakes and African Millet Bread. Recipes are given below for all of these.

Mexican tortillas are the standard 'bread' throughout Mexico and other parts of Central America, and they are just as useful for anyone on a gluten-free diet as they are made with pure cornmeal. Unfortunately, they are very difficult to make and also somewhat difficult to buy. However, Fiesta Mexican Foods Ltd of London Road, Wendover Dene, Wendover, Bucks, are importing fresh tortillas. At present they can be bought only in London at Harrods and one or two other outlets, but a stamped addressed envelope to Fiesta Foods will bring you up to date on the latest stockists. Fresh tortillas can be used on their own or to make enchiladas, tacos and the like.

There are also some very good bread substitutes on sale in specialist health food shops. One of my favourites is gluten-free Puffed Rice Cakes made from organic whole grain brown rice. Many shops now sell poppadoms and these are usually made from ground bean flour or from potato and sago flour and are therefore quite safe. They may be flavoured with garlic, black pepper or chillies. All you need to do is to deep fry or toast them over a direct flame.

White Bread

This recipe was made with a low protein non-specific gluten-free flour. The bread is very like the bought loaves.

*1 level teaspoon dried
    yeast*
1 level teaspoon sugar
*150 ml/¼ pint hand-hot
    water*
*175 g/6 oz gluten-free
    flour*

½ teaspoon salt
*50 g/2 oz dried milk
    powder*
½ tablespoon corn oil

Stir the dried yeast and sugar into the water and leave in a warm place until frothy. This takes approximately 15–20 minutes. Sift together the flour and salt into a large mixing bowl and stir in the milk powder. Stir the corn oil into the yeast liquid, add to the dry ingredients and beat to form a smooth batter. Pour into a greased and lined 450 g/1 lb loaf tin. Place inside a lightly oiled polythene bag and leave to rise in a warm place until the mixture has doubled in size, approximately 1 hour. Remove the loaf from the polythene bag and bake at 190°C/375°F/Gas 5 for 25–30 minutes until golden brown. Cool on a wire rack.

Note: If you have a wheat allergy, the non-specific gluten-free flours may not be suitable as they are usually made from wheat. Check the list of ingredients.

Crusty Bread

This bread is made with a special gluten-free flour—Trufree No 4 or No 5—and is very quick to make since it does not need to be kneaded or left to rise for very long. It can be flavoured with sesame seeds or with ground sunflower seeds. A sweet loaf can be made by stirring in 2 tablespoons of raisins and 1 tablespoon sugar.

290 g/10¼ oz Trufree No 4 or No 5 flour
1 sachet of yeast (provided with the flour)
1 tablespoon cooking oil

225 ml/8 fl oz warm water
1 tablespoon toasted sesame seeds or toasted and ground sunflower seeds (optional)

Put the flour into a bowl. Add the yeast and stir. Mix the oil and water and pour into a well in the flour. Mix to a creamy batter and add any optional flavourings. Spoon into a greased 450 g/1 lb loaf tin and leave to stand for 5 minutes. Bake at 180°C/350°F/Gas 4 for about 1 hour 10 minutes until golden brown and well risen. Turn out onto a wire rack to cool. Store in a closed polythene bag.

Buckwheat Loaf

This bread tastes very like wholemeal bread and has a good spongy texture with a crisp crust.

1 tablespoon dried yeast
1 teaspoon brown sugar
150 ml/¼ pint warm water
75 g/3 oz potato flour

50 g/2 oz maizemeal
25 g/1 oz soya flour
25 g/1 oz buckwheat flour
½ teaspoon sea salt

Mix the dried yeast, sugar and water and leave in a warm place for 15 minutes. Sift the flours into a bowl and add the salt. Stir the yeast and liquid mixture and pour onto the flour mixture. Beat well with a wooden spoon to get rid of the lumps and to give a creamy consistency. Pour into a 450 g/1 lb loaf tin and leave to stand for 5 minutes. Bake at 180°C/350°F/Gas 4 for about 1 hour until well risen and crusty. Remove from the tin and bake upside down for a further 10 minutes. Turn out onto a wire rack to cool.

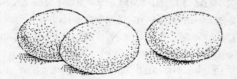

Carrot Peanut Bread

This American recipe makes a very good slicing loaf with an unusual flavour.

175 g/6 oz brown sugar
2 tablespoons chunky-style peanut butter
50 ml/2 fl oz cooking oil
2 eggs
225 g/8 oz carrots, grated
1 teaspoon vanilla essence
25 g/1 oz soya flour

50 g/2 oz fine cornmeal
75 g/3 oz coarse cornmeal or polenta
25 g/1 oz rice flour
2 teaspoons gluten-free baking powder
¼ teaspoon salt
¼ teaspoon ground allspice
¼ teaspoon grated nutmeg
100 ml/4 fl oz milk

Cream together the sugar, peanut butter, oil and eggs. Add the carrots and vanilla. Blend the flours with the baking powder, salt and spices. Add the flour mixture and the milk alternately to the carrot mixture to form a creamy dough. Turn into a greased and lined 1 kg/2 lb loaf tin (23 × 8 cm/ 9 × 3½ in). Bake at 180°C/350°F/Gas 4 for 1¼ hours until cooked through. Cover with foil after 45 minutes. Cool for 10 minutes in the tin and then remove to a wire rack to continue cooling.

Peanut Butter Cornbread

This cornbread is just as good eaten cold as hot.

125 g/5 oz *fine yellow cornmeal*
1½ teaspoons *gluten-free baking powder*
1 tablespoon *sugar*

125 g/5 oz *peanut butter*
1 egg, *beaten*
100 ml/4 fl oz *milk*
1½ tablespoons *cooking oil*

Mix together the cornmeal, baking powder and sugar. Cut in the peanut butter with a knife and then use your fingers to rub in until the mixture resembles fine breadcrumbs. Mix the egg, milk and oil and pour onto the cornmeal mixture. Stir until just blended. Pour into a 20 × 12 cm (8 × 5 in) baking tin that has been oiled and lined with baking parchment paper. Bake at 220°C/425°F/Gas 7 for 15–20 minutes.

Corn Muffins and Cornbread

This recipe can also be used to make a square loaf. Use a tin about 15 cm/6 in square and line with baking parchment paper. Serve hot with plenty of butter and jam.

1 tablespoon butter,
   cut into pieces
175 g/6 oz fine yellow
   cornmeal
½ teaspoon salt

½ teaspoon gluten-free
   baking powder
1 egg, beaten
350 ml/12 fl oz equal
   quantities buttermilk
   and milk, or all milk

Place the butter in deep bun or muffin tins or in a lined square baking tin. Mix together the cornmeal, salt and baking powder. Beat the egg with the milk and pour over dry ingredients. Stir only until just blended. Pour into the tins (or tin) and bake at 200°C/400°F/Gas 6 for 20–25 minutes. Turn out the muffins or cut the loaf into squares and serve at once.

Corn and Rice Bread

This bread may be eaten hot or cold but it should be eaten the same day that it is cooked.

175 g/6 oz fine yellow
  cornmeal
75 g/3 oz rice flour
2 teaspoons gluten-free
  baking powder

1 teaspoon salt
50 g/2 oz butter or
  firm margarine
1 egg, beaten
175–200 ml/7–8 fl oz milk

Place the cornmeal, rice flour, baking powder and salt in a bowl. Cut the fat into small pieces and rub it into the dry ingredients until the mixture resembles fine breadcrumbs. Beat the egg and milk together and then, using a wooden spoon, stir this mixture into the dry ingredients. Beat until well blended. Spoon into a greased 15 cm/6 in square baking tin. Bake at 200°C/400°F/Gas 6 for 25–30 minutes or until a skewer inserted into the centre of the cake comes out clean. Cut the cornbread into 5 cm/2 in squares and serve at once with butter.

Serbian Cornmeal Bread

This makes a very good light slicing bread.

1 tablespoon dried yeast
100 ml/4 fl oz lukewarm
  milk
1 tablespoon honey
50 g/2 oz fine yellow
  cornmeal or white
  maizemeal

25 g/1 oz potato flour
2 tablespoons soya flour
pinch salt
1 egg, beaten
1 tablespoon cooking oil

Place the yeast, milk and honey in a jug and leave in a warm place for 15–20 minutes. Place all the dry ingredients in a bowl. Beat the egg and oil together and mix with the yeast liquid. Pour onto the dry ingredients. Stir together and spoon into an oiled and lined 450 g/1 lb loaf tin. Leave in a warm place for 30 minutes. Bake at 180°C/350°F/Gas 4 for 40–45 minutes until cooked through. Leave to cool for 15–20 minutes and then place on a wire rack to cool completely.

Spoon Bread

This lovely fluffy 'bread' is served straight from the dish in which it is cooked. Serve at brunch or supper with eggs and bacon or other brunch-style grills.

350 ml/12 fl oz milk
75 g/3 oz fine yellow
   cornmeal or maizemeal
50 g/2 oz butter

1 teaspoon gluten-free
   baking powder
½ teaspoon salt
4 eggs, separated

Heat the milk in the top of a double saucepan and gradually stir in the sifted cornmeal. Add the butter and bring the mixture to the boil, stirring all the time. Remove from the heat and cool to lukewarm. Dissolve the baking powder and salt in a little more milk and beat into the mixture with the egg yolks. Whisk the egg whites until stiff and fold in. Pour into a buttered casserole and bake at 180°C/350°F/Gas 4 for 45–50 minutes, or until well puffed up and brown.

Scones

This mixture is suitable for both sweet or savoury scones. Simply substitute 50 g/2 oz strongly flavoured cheese for the sugar and raisins.

100 g/4 oz rice flour
100 g/4 oz gluten-free
   cornflour
2 teaspoons gluten-free
   baking powder
75 g/3 oz butter or
   margarine

25 g/1 oz sugar
50 g/2 oz raisins
1 egg, beaten
150 ml/¼ pint milk

Sift the flours and baking powder into a bowl and rub in the fat. Stir in the sugar and raisins and add the egg and sufficient milk to give a soft dough. Turn the mixture onto a floured surface and knead very lightly. Roll out thickly and cut into 8 scones. Brush with milk and place on a greased baking tray. Bake at 200°C/400°F/Gas 6 for 10–12 minutes. Serve hot with butter or with thick cream and jam.

African Millet Bread

This recipe comes from North Africa where millet is an important staple food. Serve for tea with butter and honey or jam or for supper with a savoury spread such as liver pâté.

1 teaspoon dried yeast
pinch sugar
*4 tablespoons lukewarm
    milk*

100 g/4 oz flaked millet
½ teaspoon salt
*225 ml/8 fl oz lukewarm
    water*

Mix the yeast and sugar with the milk and leave in a warm place for about 15 minutes. Grind the millet flakes as fine as you can get them in a food processor or grinder. Place in a bowl with the salt. Make a well in the centre and pour on the yeast and milk mixture and the water, stirring constantly with a wooden spoon to form a thin smooth batter. Beat for 1 minute and then cover the bowl with a clean cloth. Leave to stand in a warm place for 45 minutes to 1 hour until very frothy. Drop in spoonfuls onto a heated and lightly greased griddle or heavy frying pan and cook for about 5–6 minutes on each side until crisp and golden brown in colour. Keep warm while you cook the remaining batter in the same way. Serve hot.

Drop Scones or Scotch Pancakes   Makes 16–18

These drop scones have a savoury flavour and are excellent served as an accompaniment to any kind of salad or supper dish. To make sweet ones simply add a tablespoon of sugar and omit the spices. Sprinkle a few sesame seeds into either variety for a change.

100 g/4 oz gluten-free flour (Trufree No 7) or any non-specific gluten-free brand

25 g/1 oz gluten-free cornflour

1 teaspoon gluten-free baking powder

½ teaspoon salt

¼ teaspoon ground cumin or mixed spice

1 egg, beaten

8 tablespoons milk

Sift together the dry ingredients and gradually add the beaten egg and milk to give a smooth batter. Drop tablespoons of the mixture onto a heated and lightly oiled griddle or heavy frying pan. When bubbles begin to burst on the surface, turn the scones over and cook until lightly browned on both sides.

Potato Cakes

Potato cakes seem to go particularly well with boiled eggs. Cook them so that they are crispy at the edges and serve with plenty of butter.

450 g/1 lb potatoes,
   cut into chunks
40 g/1½ oz butter
2 level tablespoons
   gluten-free cornflour

3 tablespoons milk
salt and pepper

Cook the potatoes in boiling salted water for about 8–10 minutes until tender. Drain well and mash with a fork or potato masher. Beat in the butter with a fork. Mix the cornflour and milk to a smooth paste and beat into the mixture with a fork. Add seasoning. Grease a baking tray and press out the potato mixture to about 5 mm/¼ in thickness. Mark into sections with a knife and bake at the top of the oven at 190°C/375°F/Gas 5 for about 45 minutes until lightly browned and crisp at the edges. Turn up the oven to 200°C/400°F/Gas 6 for the last 10 minutes for an even crispier effect.

2

Breakfast

There are plenty of proprietary brands of breakfast cereals which are gluten-free. However, if you like muesli or porridge you will have to be more selective. In fact it is quite easy to make up your own muesli mixes and store them for use when required. If you are including nuts or seeds in the mix, do not keep it for more than a month or so or the fat in the nuts will start to go rancid.

Bread is the other staple breakfast food. Use the recipes given in the previous chapter to make loaves to slice and toast or fry.

For those who like to have a cooked breakfast and substantial brunch-style meals at the weekend, I have included some recipes which provide their own bulk, to be used instead of bread.

Mixed Cereal Muesli

Use raw grated apples, chopped pears or halved and pipped grapes in season. This quantity makes enough for 4 people, but you could make up larger quantities of the dry ingredients and store in an airtight jar for up to a month.

4 tablespoons flaked rice
4 tablespoons flaked millet
2 tablespoons soya flakes
1 tablespoon sunflower seeds
1 tablespoon flaked brazil nuts
8 walnut halves, chopped
1 tablespoon raisins
225 ml/8 fl oz water or milk
fruit to taste
4 tablespoons plain yogurt

Mix all the dry ingredients and leave in a large bowl or spoon into four individual bowls. Pour on the water or milk. Cover and leave to stand overnight. In the morning top with fruit and yogurt. If you like a more runny muesli, add some more water or milk and stir the muesli before adding the fruit and yogurt.

Millet and Hazelnut Muesli

This is a much smoother muesli than the mixed cereal muesli but the hazelnuts give added interest. This makes enough for 4 servings.

6 tablespoons flaked
  millet
4 tablespoons flaked
  rice
2 tablespoons chopped
  toasted hazelnuts
1 teaspoon chopped
  stoned dates
1 teaspoon toasted
  sesame seeds
225 ml/8 fl oz water
  or milk
fruit to taste
4 tablespoons plain
  yogurt

Mix all the dry ingredients and leave in a large bowl or spoon into individual bowls. Pour on the water or milk. Cover and leave to stand overnight. In the morning top with fruit and yogurt. If you like a more runny muesli, add some more water or milk and stir the muesli before adding the fruit and yogurt.

Crunchy Breakfast Rice

2 tablespoons flaked rice
2 tablespoons flaked
   almonds

3–4 tablespoons rice
   crispies per person
milk and sugar to taste

Place the rice flakes and flaked almonds in the bottom of the grill pan and toast for 2–3 minutes, stirring from time to time until lightly browned and crisp. Alternatively dry fry in a heavy non-stick frying pan. Leave to cool.

Spoon the rice crispies into four bowls. Sprinkle with the toasted rice and almond mixture and serve with milk and sugar to taste.

Breakfast Yogurt

4 tablespoons flaked
  millet
4 tablespoons flaked
  Brazil nuts
275 g/10 oz plain
  yogurt
brown sugar to taste

225 g/8 oz sieved and
  puréed apples, dried
  apricots or prunes
50 g/2 oz green or black
  grapes, halved and
  pipped

Place the millet and Brazil nuts in the grill pan and toast, stirring from time to time, until browned. Alternatively, dry fry in a heavy non-stick pan until browned. Leave to cool. Mix with the yogurt and sugar to taste.

Spoon the sieved fruit into four individual bowls. Top with the crunchy yogurt mixture and decorate with grapes.

Rice and Millet Porridge

Both flaked rice and flaked millet make quite good porridge. However, the taste is not as good as oat porridge and it needs to be flavoured well.

50 g/2 oz flaked rice or flaked millet
300 ml/½ pint equal quantities milk and water

1–2 tablespoons brown sugar

Flavourings:
1½ teaspoons ground cinnamon
1 tablespoon raisins or chopped apricots

2 tablespoons honey in place of the sugar

Place the flaked cereal in the top half of a double saucepan. Add the liquid and sugar and place over gently simmering water. Cook the porridge for about 5–8 minutes, stirring all the time. The longer you cook the porridge the thicker it will become. Add your chosen flavourings just before serving.

Fried Polenta Squares with Poached Eggs

Fried polenta makes an excellent substitute for fried bread.

900 ml/1½ pints water
175 g/6 oz coarse yellow
  cornmeal or polenta

1 teaspoon salt
4 eggs
cooking oil

Bring the water to the boil in a saucepan and add the cornmeal and salt in a thin but steady stream, beating all the time with a wooden spoon to avoid lumps. Reduce the heat and simmer for 20–30 minutes, stirring frequently. When the polenta is cooked it will come easily off the sides of the pan. Turn onto a wooden board and knead into a square about 3 cm/1½ in thick. Leave to cool and cut into 4 squares.

Poach the eggs in a very lightly greased egg poacher or in water with a dash of vinegar and keep warm. Heat a little oil in a frying pan and fry the polenta squares until golden on each side. Serve with an egg on top of each slice.

Potato Pancakes with Mushrooms

Use leftover mashed potatoes for Mixture 1 and the pancakes will be ready very quickly indeed. Grill the mushrooms, sprinkled with the same seasonings, if you are watching your fat intake.

Pancake Mixture 1

*350 g/12 oz mashed
  potatoes
2 tablespoons potato
  flour*

*1 egg, beaten
salt and pepper
gluten-free cornflour
cooking oil*

Mix the mashed potato with the potato flour and half the egg. Season to taste and shape into 4 cakes. Coat with the remaining egg and some cornflour and fry in hot oil until crisp and brown on each side. This takes about 3–4 minutes.

Pancake Mixture 2

450 g/1 lb potatoes,
    grated
1 small onion, finely
    chopped

1 small egg, beaten
salt and pepper

Squeeze the liquid out of the potatoes and onion and mix with the egg and seasoning. Drop in spoonfuls onto a hot pan and cook gently, covered, for 10 minutes on each side.

Mushroom Topping

225 g/8 oz mushrooms,
    sliced
50 g/2 oz butter

1/4 teaspoon dried thyme
1/4 teaspoon garlic salt
pepper

Gently fry the mushrooms in the butter to soften them. Add the herbs and seasonings and cook for about 5 minutes. Serve on top of the cooked potato pancakes.

Corn and Apple Pancakes

Makes 8

These small thick pancakes can be served with bacon and egg or with butter and maple syrup or honey.

50 g/2 oz cornmeal –
   yellow or white
50 g/2 oz rice flour
1 teaspoon gluten-free
   baking powder
1 egg, beaten
150 ml/¼ pint milk

2 small apples, peeled and
   grated
2 tablespoons sweetcorn
   kernels
1 tablespoon sugar
cooking oil for frying

Beat the cornmeal, rice flour and baking powder with the egg and sufficient milk to make a fairly thick batter. Stir in the grated apples, sweetcorn and sugar. Drop in spoonfuls onto a heated and very lightly greased griddle or heavy frying pan. Cook very gently for about 5–10 minutes on each side until puffed up and golden in colour. Test to see that they are cooked through and cook for a little longer if necessary.

Rice and Coddled Eggs

This makes a quick breakfast 'scramble' with the cereal or bulk content incorporated into the one dish. Use brown rice for a higher nutritional value. This will need to be cooked for 10–15 minutes longer in the initial stages.

175 g/6 oz long grain rice
1 teaspoon salt

350 ml/12 fl oz water
2 eggs, beaten
pepper

Optional flavourings:
50 g/2 oz cooked ham, diced
2 tablespoons freshly chopped parsley

50 g/2 oz cooked peas

Topping:
2 tomatoes, finely chopped

pinch chilli powder

Place the rice in a pan with the salt and water and bring to the boil. Stir once and cover with a lid. Reduce the heat and simmer for about 12 minutes until almost dry. Pour the eggs onto the rice, sprinkle with pepper and stir well. Return to a very low heat and continue cooking for 2–3 minutes. Stir in your chosen flavouring and heat through. Mix the chopped tomatoes with chilli powder to taste and serve on top of the rice.

Eggy Bread

Use bought gluten-free bread or one of the sliceable breads given in Chapter 1. Crusty Bread, Serbian Cornmeal Bread or Buckwheat Loaf are all suitable. Serve with grilled tomatoes.

1 egg, beaten
1 tablespoon milk
salt and pepper
4 slices gluten-free
* bread* (small loaf)

butter or cooking oil
* for frying*

Mix together the egg, milk and seasoning in a soup bowl. Dip the slices of bread in this mixture and leave until well coated. Heat a non-stick frying pan and brush with a very little butter or oil. Fry the eggy bread for about 2–3 minutes on each side until crisp and golden.

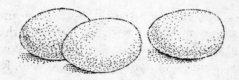

3
Soup

A good soup really needs a good stock as its base but nowadays this is no problem. There are plenty of stock cubes on the market and most of the leading brands are gluten-free though to be sure you should check against the Coeliac Society's list of gluten-free manufactured products.

Though stock cubes are convenient they do not always taste the same as the real thing and for a really good Chicken Noodle Soup I believe that there is nothing to beat a broth made with a good boiling fowl. The noodles will not present a problem either for I have used Chinese transparent or cellophane noodles (see page 52) made from bean flour. You could also use Chinese rice noodles (see page 52).

Chinese Chicken Noodle Soup

This is almost a meal in itself!

2 large spring onions,
  chopped
2.5 cm/1 in fresh root
  ginger, finely chopped
1 clove garlic (optional)
1 tablespoon cooking oil
½ boiling fowl or 2
  chicken joints, cut
  into 4–6 pieces

salt and pepper
50 g/2 oz water
  transparent or
  cellophane noodles,
  soaked in hot water
  for 5 minutes
175 g/6 oz Chinese
  cabbage, cut into
  5 mm/¼ in slices

Fry the spring onions, ginger and garlic in the oil for 1–2 minutes. Add the chicken to the pan and cover with boiling water. Bring to the boil and season. Cover and simmer for 1 hour. Remove the chicken pieces and continue boiling the liquid to reduce it to 1 litre/1¾ pints. Meanwhile, skin and bone the chicken and cut the meat into strips. Return to the soup with the noodles and cabbage. Return to the boil, simmer for 3 minutes and serve.

Scotch Broth with Whole Millet

Scotch Broth traditionally includes pearl barley. Here I have substituted whole millet. The effect is a little different as the millet does not retain the bite that pearl barley does. For a soup with a lower fat content use chicken joints in place of lamb.

450 g/1 lb scrag end
   neck of lamb
1 tablespoon cooking oil
1 large onion, chopped
1 large carrot, chopped
3 sticks celery, chopped

1 potato, diced
1 bay leaf
pinch dried thyme
salt and pepper
15 g/½ oz whole millet

Cut off as much surface fat as possible from the lamb. Place in a large saucepan and cover with water. Bring to the boil, cover and simmer for 1 hour. Remove the meat and leave the liquid to cool. Remove the fat from the top of the liquid, and take the meat from the bones. Heat the oil in another saucepan and fry the onion until it turns transparent. Add the remaining vegetables and fry gently for 3–4 minutes. Make the lamb stock up to 900 ml/1½ pints with water and add to the pan with the meat from the bones, the herbs and seasoning. Bring to the boil, cover and simmer for 1 hour. Add the millet and simmer for a further 12 minutes until the millet is tender. Serve at once.

Millet Soup with Cheese

1 onion, very finely
  chopped
25 g/1 oz butter
2 tablespoons freshly
  chopped parsley
50 g/2 oz whole millet
450 ml/³⁄4 pint milk

450 ml/³⁄4 pint chicken
  stock
salt and pepper
50 g/2 oz Gruyère or
  Emmenthal cheese,
  grated

Fry the onion very gently in the butter to soften it. Add the parsley and millet. Pour on the milk and chicken stock and season. Bring to the boil and simmer for 35–40 minutes. Serve sprinkled with the grated cheese.

Thick soups

There are plenty of ways of thickening soups without using a gluten flour. The simplest is to use a little gluten-free cornflour mixed to a smooth paste with water. This is stirred into the cooked soup and the soup is brought to the boil. However, the cornflour does tend to taste. This can be counteracted to some extent by continuing to cook the soup for about 5 minutes after the cornflour has been added.

Another way of thickening soups is to include some starchy ingredients such as potatoes or beans and then to purée the soup after cooking. This results in a thick, hearty soup which does not need any extra thickening. Here are two typical recipes. Simply change the flavouring vegetables to give quite different soups.

Carrot and Potato Soup

For a complete change of flavour use cauliflower, parsnips,
celeriac or broccoli in place of carrots.

1 large onion, sliced
1 tablespoon cooking oil
3 tablespoons sherry
450 g/1 lb carrots, sliced
225 g/8 oz (1 large)
* potato, chopped*

900 ml/1½ pints vegetable
* stock*
salt and pepper
pinch curry powder
* (optional)*

Fry the onion in the cooking oil until lightly browned. Add
the sherry and bring to the boil. Add all the remaining
ingredients and return to the boil. Simmer for 1 hour. Purée
in a food processor or blender or rub through a sieve.
Reheat and serve.

Pulse and Pepper Soup

For a change of flavour use 225 g/8 oz green cabbage or 1 large head fennel in place of the pepper.

1 large onion, sliced
1 tablespoon cooking oil
1 green pepper, seeded
    and sliced
50 g/2 oz split lentils
50 g/2 oz dried haricot
    or black eye beans,
    soaked in boiling water
    for 2 hours

900 ml/1 ½ pints meat or
    chicken stock
½ teaspoon dried mixed
    herbs
salt and pepper

Fry the onion in the oil with the green pepper until lightly browned. Add the lentils, the drained beans and the stock. Bring to the boil and add the herbs. Cook for 1 hour until the beans are tender. Add seasoning to taste. Purée in a blender or food processor or rub through a sieve. Reheat and serve.

Cream of Courgette Soup

For special occasion soups a mixture of egg yolk and cream can be used to thicken a delicate soup. Use courgettes, lettuce, watercress, leeks or fennel in this cream soup.

1 onion, sliced
15 g/½ oz butter
2 tablespoons sherry
450 g/1 lb courgettes, sliced
600 ml/1 pint chicken or vegetable stock
pinch dill weed or marjoram

salt and pepper
1 egg yolk
3 tablespoons double cream
freshly chopped parsley, to garnish

Gently fry the onion in the butter until it turns transparent. Add the sherry and bring to the boil. Next add the courgettes, stock, herbs and seasoning. Return to the boil and simmer for 30 minutes. Purée in a blender or food processor or rub through a sieve. Beat the egg yolk and cream together and pour into the puréed soup. Reheat gently, stirring all the time. Do not allow the mixture to boil. Serve garnished with a little chopped parsley.

Watercress Soup

Cereals, such as rice, can also be used to thicken soup.

2 bunches watercress,
washed
50 g/2 oz long-grain rice
600 ml/1 pint milk

300 ml/½ pint water
salt and pepper
2 tablespoons cream

Place the watercress in a saucepan with the rice, milk and water. Season. Bring to the boil and simmer for 25 minutes. Purée in a blender or food processor. Stir in the cream. Reheat and serve.

4

Soufflés and Savoury Dishes

There are of course many, many savoury dishes which do not use flour or breadcrumbs, but if a particular dish is 'off-limits' you are bound to get a craving for it!

The recipes below set out to solve a few of those problem areas.

Soufflés

These light and fluffy concoctions can be made with gluten-free flour or rather more cheaply with rice, millet or potatoes used in its place.

Cheese and Rice Soufflé

This makes a well-flavoured and very light soufflé.

100 g/4 oz flaked millet
  or rice
600 ml/1 pint milk
175 g/6 oz Cheddar
  cheese, grated

4 eggs, separated
1 teaspoon salt

Cook the flakes in the milk in the top of a double saucepan for 10–15 minutes until the mixture is thick. Remove from the heat. Beat in the cheese, egg yolks and salt. Whisk the whites until stiff. Stir a tablespoonful into the flake and cheese mixture and then fold in the rest. Spoon into a greased soufflé dish and bake at 200°C/400°F/Gas 6 for 30–35 minutes until well risen and set in the centre. Serve at once.

Quick Cheese Soufflé

It is possible to make a very good cheese soufflé with no thickening agent at all. However, it must be served immediately it is cooked as it flops even more quickly than an ordinary soufflé.

4 eggs, separated
100 g/4 oz Cheddar
    cheese, grated

pinch each of paprika
    and celery salt
black pepper

Mix the egg yolks with the cheese and seasonings. Whisk the egg whites until they are really stiff. Stir a tablespoonful into the cheese mixture and then quickly fold in the rest. Spoon into a greased soufflé dish and bake at 190°C/375°F/Gas 5 for 40–45 minutes until well puffed up and set in the centre. Serve at once.

Chicken Soufflé

This makes a slightly larger, very fluffy soufflé. Halve quantities for a starter or for 2 people.

25 g/1 oz rice flour
25 g/1 oz gluten-free cornflour
150 ml/¼ pint chicken stock
200 ml/7 fl oz milk

25 g/1 oz butter
300 g/10 oz cooked chicken meat, finely chopped
salt and pepper
6 eggs, separated

Mix the rice flour and cornflour to a smooth paste with a little of the chicken stock. Stir in the rest of the stock and the milk and transfer to a saucepan. Stir in the butter and bring to the boil over a low heat, stirring all the time. Cook for 1 minute. Remove from the heat. Add the chicken, seasoning and egg yolks. Whisk the egg whites until they are very stiff and stir a tablespoonful into the chicken mixture. Fold in the rest of the egg whites and spoon into a large soufflé dish. Bake at 200°C/400°F/Gas 6 for 30–35 minutes, until the soufflé is well risen and is set in the centre. Serve at once.

Potato-based Soufflé

This mixture is not quite as light as the other soufflés but is quick to make and useful if you do not have any special flours to hand. Flavour with diced chicken or sautéed mushrooms in place of cheese.

450 g/1 lb potatoes,
chopped
50 g/2 oz butter
4–5 tablespoons milk
100 g/4 oz Cheddar
cheese, grated, or
blue cheese, chopped

salt and pepper
5 eggs, separated

Cook the potatoes in boiling salted water until tender. Drain very well and mash with the butter and milk. Beat well. Stir in the cheese, seasoning and egg yolks. Whisk the egg whites until they are really stiff. Stir 2 tablespoonfuls into the potato mixture and then fold in the rest. Spoon into a greased soufflé dish and bake at 200°C/400°F/Gas 6 for 25–30 minutes.

Thickened Casseroles

Casseroles can be thickened with corn-based products such as gluten-free cornflour or maize flour but this tends to give a slightly gluey effect to the gravy. They also have to be mixed with a little liquid before adding to the mixture to be thickened and can easily go lumpy.

Brown and Polson are test-marketing a product called One-step which thickens stews and casseroles by simply sprinkling it over and stirring in. It is expected to be nationally available shortly.

Alternatives are to use instant dried mashed potato powder or peanut butter or simply to purée the vegetables and liquid with which the meat has been cooked. Here are some recipes demonstrating these other methods.

Chicken à la Moambe

If you like peanut butter you will love the rich sauce in this top-of-the-stove chicken casserole.

4 chicken joints, skinned and cut into pieces
2 tablespoons cooking oil
2 tablespoons tomato purée

300 ml/½ pint water, or equal quantities water and white wine
salt and pepper
2 tablespoons peanut butter

Fry the chicken pieces in hot cooking oil to seal and brown them. Drain off all the oil. Mix the tomato purée with the water and seasoning and pour over the chicken. Bring to the boil, then cover with a lid and simmer for 30–35 minutes until the chicken is tender. Remove the chicken pieces from the pan and keep warm. Stir the peanut butter into the cooking juices and bring to the boil, stirring all the time. Arrange the chicken on a serving plate and pour the sauce over the top.

Chicken in Red Wine

This makes a really warming family stew. For special occasions increase the wine and use less stock.

1 large onion, sliced
1 tablespoon cooking oil
1 carrot, sliced
2 sticks celery, chopped
4 chicken joints, skinned and cut in half

150 ml/¼ pint chicken stock
150 ml/¼ pint red wine
1 bouquet garni
salt and pepper
1½ tablespoons instant dried mashed potato powder

Fry the onion in the cooking oil in a frying pan until it starts to brown. Add the carrot and celery and continue frying more gently for 3–4 minutes. Remove the vegetables from the pan with a slotted spoon and place in a casserole. Fry the pieces of chicken in the oil until well sealed and lightly browned. Add to the vegetables in the casserole and stir. Pour on the stock and red wine and add the bouquet garni and seasoning. Cook at 180°C/350°F/Gas 4 for 45 minutes. Sprinkle with the potato powder and stir in. Cook for a further half hour, adding a little more potato at the end if necessary.

Monkfish with Vegetable Sauce

The vegetables in the sauce form the thickening and this effect can be enhanced by puréeing the sauce just before serving.

700 g/1½ lb monkfish
  fillets, cut into
  large pieces
15 g/½ oz butter
1 tablespoon olive oil
1 large onion, finely
  chopped
2 carrots, grated
2 sticks celery, finely
  chopped
450 g/1 lb tomatoes,
  skinned, seeded and
  chopped

1 tablespoon tomato
  purée
150 ml/¼ pint chicken
  stock
150 ml/¼ pint dry
  white wine
salt and pepper
2.5 cm/1 in strip lemon
  peel (optional)

Garnish:

2 tablespoons freshly
  chopped parsley
grated lemon rind

1 clove garlic, very
  finely chopped
(optional)

Fry the fish in the butter and oil to seal, then remove with a slotted spoon. Gently cook the vegetables in the remaining fat. Add the tomato purée, stock, wine, seasoning and lemon peel and stir well. Return the fish to the pan. Cover and bring to the boil. Simmer for about 30 minutes until the vegetables are tender. Transfer the fish to a serving dish. Discard the lemon peel, if liked. Purée the sauce in a blender or food processor or rub through a sieve and pour over the fish. Serve sprinkled with the garnish.

Cod Lyonnaise

The potatoes in this dish give it substance. Serve with a green salad on the side.

2 onions, chopped
1 tablespoon cooking oil
2 rashers streaky bacon,
 rinds removed and
 chopped (optional)
1 kg/2 lb potatoes, diced
1 tomato, skinned and
 chopped

450 g/1 lb boneless
 white fish (cod,
 haddock, huss or
 coley), cut into
 chunks
150 ml/¼ pint milk
salt and pepper

Fry the onions in the cooking oil until they turn transparent. Add the bacon, if using, and fry for a further 1–2 minutes. Add all the remaining ingredients and bring to the boil. Reduce the heat, cover and simmer for 30 minutes or until the potatoes are soft.

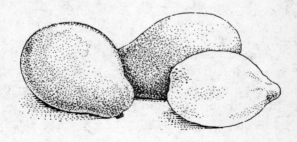

Vegetable Curry with Chickpeas

Most curries are thickened by the reduction of the cooking juices and this recipe is no exception. Chickpeas give extra body and protein.

2.5 cm/1 in fresh root ginger, finely chopped
1 clove garlic, crushed
1 teaspoon whole cumin seeds
6 black peppercorns
2 cloves
2 cardamom pods
2 tablespoons cooking oil
1 onion, chopped
2 tablespoons mild curry powder

1 large potato, diced
½ head small cauliflower, cut into florets
100 g/4 oz green peas
175 g/6 oz canned chickpeas
175 g/6 oz any other vegetable in season
125 g/5 oz plain yogurt
salt and pepper
2 tomatoes, cut into quarters

Fry the ginger, garlic, cumin, peppercorns, cloves and cardamom in the cooking oil for 1 minute to bring out the flavour. Add the onion and curry powder and continue frying for a further 2–3 minutes, stirring well. Add all the vegetables and stir to coat well with the spices. Pour on the yogurt and season. Cook gently for 45–50 minutes, stirring from time to time, until the curry thickens. Add the tomato quarters after about 45 minutes, and leave to rest off the heat for 5 minutes before serving.

Rice and Vegetable Pie

100 g/4 oz long-grain
   rice
200 ml/8 fl oz boiling
   water
salt and pepper
1 small onion, finely
   chopped
1 tablespoon cooking oil

4 courgettes, sliced
½ red pepper, seeded
   and chopped
100 g/4 oz Cheddar
   cheese, grated
2 tablespoons crushed
   cornflakes

Cook the rice in the boiling salted water for about 12–15 minutes until the rice is tender and all the liquid has been absorbed. Meanwhile, fry the onion in the cooking oil until it turns transparent. Add the courgettes and red pepper and continue frying gently for about 10 minutes until the vegetables are tender. Grease a casserole dish and press half the cooked rice into the bottom. Top with the vegetables and three-quarters of the cheese. Spread the remaining rice over the top. Mix the rest of the cheese with the crushed cornflakes and sprinkle over the top. Bake at 190°C/375°F/Gas 5 for 20–30 minutes. Serve with salad.

Pasta

Both Italian pasta and Chinese egg noodles are made from wheat. However, if you can get to a specialist Chinese or Japanese grocer you will be able to have some gluten-free pasta or noodle dishes.

There are three types of noodles on sale which are suitable for a gluten-free diet. They are:

Transparent or cellophane noodles: These are made from mung bean flour. They may be labelled funsee or Hankow vermicelli.

Rice noodles: These are made from rice flour. They come in a variety of thicknesses and are quite versatile. They may be labelled hor fun, mi fun, thai mee or rice sticks.

Buckwheat noodles: These are made from buckwheat flour but need to be treated with more care than the previous two for they may contain some wheat and it is usually impossible to read the ingredients!

Here are some recipes using these noodles.

Note: Soy sauce contains wheat but Sunwheel Japanese tamari sauce, which is very similar, does not.

Rice Noodles with Prawns and Fennel

225 g/8 oz rice noodles
2 onions, sliced
2 small heads fennel,
  sliced
100 g/4 oz button
  mushrooms, sliced
½ red or green pepper,
  seeded and sliced
2 tablespoons cooking oil
150 ml/¼ pint water

2 tablespoons sherry
2 tablespoons Japanese
  tamari sauce
¼ teaspoon five spice
  powder
salt and pepper
225 g/8 oz cooked peeled
  prawns
50 g/2 oz bean sprouts

Place the noodles in a heatproof bowl and cover with boiling water. Leave to stand for 30 minutes. Drain and keep on one side. Fry the onions, fennel, mushrooms and pepper in the oil for 1 minute. Add the water, sherry, tamari sauce, five spice powder and seasoning and bring to the boil. Simmer for 2 minutes, then add the drained noodles. Continue cooking until almost all the liquid has been taken up. Stir in the prawns and bean sprouts. Toss well to heat through and serve at once.

Crispy Noodles with Sweet and Sour Pork

Both rice and bean noodles crisp up beautifully when deep fried. Rice noodles have perhaps just the edge for flavour.

450 g/1 lb lean pork,
  cubed
25 g/1 oz gluten-free
  cornflour
2 teaspoons salt
pinch gluten-free baking
  powder

2 eggs, beaten
cooking oil for deep
  frying
1 jar Sharwood's Sweet
  and Sour Sauce, heated
100 g/4 oz rice noodles
  or transparent noodles

Toss the pork in the cornflour, salt and baking powder until well coated. Dip in egg and toss in the cornflour mixture again. Deep fry for 2–3 minutes in batches of 6 or 8 pieces. Recrisp the balls again in hot fat and glaze with the heated sauce. Toss the noodles, about one-eighth at a time, into the hot fat and remove with a slotted spoon. Drain on kitchen paper and serve with the pork.

Stir-fried Chicken with Transparent Noodles

100 g/4 oz transparent
or cellophane noodles
5 cm/2 in fresh root
ginger, cut into thin
sticks
3 tablespoons cooking oil
300 g/10 oz chicken meat,
cut into thin strips
2 onions, sliced

225 g/8 oz French beans,
topped and tailed
½ red pepper, seeded
and cut into strips
175 g/6 oz Chinese
leaves, shredded
3 tablespoons Japanese
tamari sauce
salt and pepper

Place the noodles in a bowl and cover with boiling water. Leave to stand for 5 minutes and drain well. Fry the ginger in 2 tablespoons of oil and add the chicken strips. Stir-fry for 1–2 minutes until there is no more pink colour on the meat. Remove the chicken from the pan and keep on one side. Add the remaining oil to the pan and stir-fry the onions, beans and pepper for 1 minute. Add the Chinese leaves and continue stir-frying for a further minute. Add the noodles and the tamari to the pan and turn up the heat. Toss until the mixture is fairly dry. Add the cooked chicken and seasoning. Continue tossing over the heat for a further minute. Serve at once.

5
Snacks and Canapés

There are plenty of snacks and canapé recipes which do not use cereals and for those that do specify toast or fried bread most of the bread recipes given in Chapter 1 can be pressed into service.

For canapé bases fry slices of Crusty Bread with sesame seeds (see page 8) or Carrot Peanut Bread (see page 10) and top with liver pâté, cream cheese and chives or scrambled eggs flavoured with smoked fish. Brown Rice Snaps, on sale in health food shops, also make a very good base for a selection of cocktail canapés. Incidently, both these and the Puffed Rice Cakes mentioned in Chapter 1 are very useful to serve with a cheese board.

Cornmeal Balls

Makes 10–12

These deliciously crumbly cheese balls make excellent cocktail canapés.

150 ml/¼ pint water
½ teaspoon salt
75 g/3 oz maizemeal

75 g/3 oz Edam cheese,
*   grated*
oil for deep frying

Place the water and salt in a saucepan and bring to boiling point. Gradually stir in the maizemeal. When thoroughly blended cook for 5 minutes, stirring constantly. The mixture will come away from the bottom and sides of the pan. Remove from the heat and stir in the cheese.

When cool enough to handle, shape spoonfuls into balls and then into cigar shapes. Deep fry until golden brown and drain on kitchen paper.

Stuffed Tacos

Ready-made tacos are fairly easy to find on the supermarket shelves. They are made only from corn. However, the seasoning mixes may contain some flour so check with the manufacturer or dispense with them and make up your own spicing.

Stuffed Tacos make an excellent snack meal. Allow about 4 per person. Serve them instead of on-toast items for quick lunches or television suppers. Choose one or two fillings and a sauce and add shredded lettuce below the filling and grated cheese on top. The flat enchiladas can be used in much the same way; simply build up in layers. Tacos are usually crisper and have a better flavour if they are heated in the oven just before serving.

Here are some Mexican-style fillings. Tacos are also very good with scrambled eggs, baked beans and bacon or cold cottage cheese and salad.

Fillings:

Spicy Minced Beef

1 large onion, chopped
1 tablespoon cooking oil
1 clove garlic, crushed
  (optional)
1–2 green chillies,
  seeded and chopped
350 g/12 oz lean minced
  beef

1 teaspoon gluten-free
  cornflour
1–2 tablespoons water
1 tablespoon tomato
  purée
pinch ground cumin
salt and pepper

Fry the onion in the oil until soft and add the garlic and chilli. Continue frying until the onion is lightly browned. Stir in the beef and brown all over. Mix the cornflour and water and stir in with all the remaining ingredients. Bring to the boil, stirring all the time. Reduce the heat and simmer for 30–40 minutes until the filling is thick and well cooked.

Cheese Straws   Makes 20–25

75 g/3 oz rice flour
50 g/2 oz gluten-free
  cornflour
50 g/2 oz medium
  cornmeal or polenta

½ teaspoon salt
100 g/4 oz butter
75 g/3 oz strong-flavoured
  hard cheese, grated

Place the flours, cornmeal and salt in a bowl and mix well together. Add the butter cut into small pieces. Rub the fat into the dry ingredients until the mixture resembles fine breadcrumbs. Stir in the cheese and add a little water to bind to a stiff dough. Roll out to about 5 mm/¼ in thick and cut into straws. Place on a greased baking tray and bake at 200°C/400°F/Gas 6 for 12–15 minutes until crisp and golden.

Refried Beans

1 large onion, thinly
  sliced
2 tablespoons cooking oil
1 × 400 g/14 oz can red
  kidney beans, well
  drained

salt and pepper
1 tablespoon freshly
  chopped parsley

Fry the sliced onion in the cooking oil until well browned.
Add the beans and bash them with the end of a wooden
spoon to break them down a little. Season and fry on both
sides until well browned. Sprinkle with parsley and break
up with a fork to use as a filling.

Chicken with Avocado

1 onion, finely chopped
1 green chilli, seeded
  and chopped
1 tablespoon cooking oil
1 tomato, peeled and
  chopped
grated rind and juice
  of 1 lime or ½ lemon

225 g/8 oz cooked
  chicken meat, diced
1 large avocado, peeled,
  stoned and cubed
1–2 tablespoons double
  cream (optional)
salt and pepper

Fry the onion and chilli in the cooking oil until the onion
turns transparent. Add the tomato, lime or lemon rind and
juice and the chicken and heat through over a low heat. Add
the avocado, cream and seasoning. Bring to the boil and
cook for a further 1–2 minutes before seasoning.

Sauces:

Tomato Sauce

For a much hotter sauce, seed and chop the chillies and cook with the onions. This sauce can also be served uncooked. Simply purée the ingredients in a blender or food processor. Use seeded chillies for the uncooked sauce.

1 small onion, chopped
1–2 whole green chillies
1 tablespoon cooking oil
450 g/1 lb tomatoes,
chopped
grated rind and juice
of 1 lime or ½ lemon

1 tablespoon freshly
chopped coriander or
¼ teaspoon ground
coriander
2 tablespoons tomato
purée
salt and pepper

Fry the onion and green chillies in the cooking oil until the onion turns translucent. Add all the remaining ingredients and bring to the boil. Cook for 20–30 minutes. Remove the whole chillies and purée in a blender or food processor or rub through a sieve. Reheat to serve.

Guacamole Sauce

1 large avocado,
   peeled and stoned
juice of 1½ lemons
salt

few drops Tabasco
   sauce
1 tablespoon grated
   onion

Purée the avocado with the lemon juice and stir in the remaining ingredients. Chill for 30 minutes before serving.

Buckwheat Pancakes Stuffed with Spiced Potatoes

These pancakes can be used with all kinds of savoury fillings. Make in advance and store in the fridge until required.

Pancakes:

25 g/1 oz buckwheat

25 g/1 oz rice flour

50 g/2 oz gluten-free cornflour

salt

1 egg

150 ml/¼ pint milk

Filling:

450 g/1 lb potatoes, cubed

1 teaspoon whole cumin seeds

½ teaspoon whole coriander seeds

2 tablespoons cooking oil

1 teaspoon turmeric

seeds from 3 cardamom pods

1 onion, sliced

Mix the flours in a bowl with the salt. Add the egg and milk and stir well. Leave to stand for 15 minutes and stir again. Place 2 or 3 spoonfuls in a hot, lightly greased frying pan and cook for 1 minute or so until lightly browned. Turn over and cook on the other side. Keep warm while you cook the remaining pancakes.

To make the filling, fry the cumin and coriander seeds in the hot oil for about ½ minute. Stir in the turmeric, cardamom seeds and the onion. Fry until the onion is lightly browned. Meanwhile, cook the potato in boiling salted water until almost tender. Drain and add to the pan with the onions and spices. Toss over the heat until the potatoes are well mixed in. Use to stuff the pancakes.

Savoury Rice Fritters

300 ml/½ pint milk
50 g/2 oz pudding rice
1 cardamom pod, crushed
2 small (size 6) eggs,
  beaten
1 hard-boiled egg,
  chopped

50 g/2 oz peas, cooked
salt and pepper
75 g/3 oz rice crispies,
  crushed
cooking oil

Place the milk and pudding rice in the top half of a double saucepan and add the cardamom. Pour about 7.5 cm/3 in water into the bottom half and bring to the boil. Reduce the heat and cover the top half with a lid. Simmer for 1½ hours until the mixture is really thick. Stir from time to time. Stir in one of the beaten eggs and remove from the heat. Add the hard-boiled egg and peas and season. Leave the mixture to cool, then chill for 1 hour. Shape the mixture into small cakes or fritters. Dip in the remaining beaten egg and coat with crushed rice crispies. Fry on both sides in hot cooking oil and serve at once.

6

Stuffings and Coatings

All kinds of stuffings and coatings can be made with crumbs from the various breads made in Chapter 1. However, it's good to have a change sometimes and here are some recipes which do not depend upon any kind of bread.

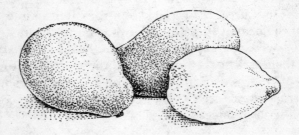

Stuffings:

Chestnut Stuffing from Turkey

75 g/3 oz long-grain
   rice
175 ml/6 fl oz boiling
   water
salt
½ × 439 g/15 oz can whole
   chestnuts in brine,
   well drained and
   chopped

1 large onion, finely
   chopped
1 tablespoon cooking oil
2 eggs, beaten
pepper
½ teaspoon mixed herbs
little grated
   lemon rind

Add the rice to the boiling salted water. Stir once, cover with a lid and simmer for 12–15 minutes until all the liquid has been absorbed and the grains of rice are tender. Grind coarsely in a food processor and mix with the chestnuts. Keep on one side. Fry the onion in the cooking oil for 3–4 minutes until soft. Stir into the rice and chestnut mixture with all the remaining ingredients. Use to stuff into the turkey, or bake in an earthenware dish on its own for 1 hour at 190°C/375°F/Gas 5.

Sage and Onion Stuffing for Chicken

25 g/1 oz flaked rice or millet
75 ml/3 fl oz chicken stock

2 large onions, chopped
2 teaspoons dried sage
salt and pepper
1 egg, beaten

Cook the rice or millet flakes in the top of a double saucepan with the chicken stock. Stir from time to time and cook until the mixture thickens. Meanwhile, cook the onions in water for 4–5 minutes to soften them. Drain very well and mix with the cooked rice or millet and the remaining ingredients. Use to stuff the chicken, or spoon into a small earthenware dish and bake on its own.

Vegetarian Stuffing for Vegetables

100 g/4 oz soya bean
   flakes
1 tablespoon flaked rice
   or millet
1 tablespoon ground
   almonds

175 ml/6 fl oz milk,
   heated to just below
   boiling
2 eggs, beaten
salt and pepper
½ teaspoon dried savory

Place the soya bean flakes, rice or millet flakes and ground almonds in a bowl and pour on the hot milk. Leave to stand for 15 minutes. Beat in the remaining ingredients and spoon into prepared green peppers, hollowed-out aubergines or courgettes or wrap in blanched cabbage leaves. Bake at 180°C/350°F/Gas 4 for about 45 minutes until the vegetables are tender and the filling is set.

Coatings:

The following ingredients make excellent coatings for shallow fried rissoles, fish cakes or croquettes. For deep frying roll the item in beaten egg and then in your chosen coating.

Crushed rice crispies
Crushed cornflakes
Ground flaked millet
Ground flaked rice
Equal quantities of rice flour and gluten-free cornflour

The first two give a darker coating than the other three. Most of these coatings can also be used to bake food in the oven. Some more ideas are included below.

Deep Fried Potato Balls

450 g/1 lb potatoes,
  cubed
75 g/3 oz well-flavoured
  hard cheese, grated
50 g/2 oz breadcrumbs,
  made from Crusty Bread
  or Buckwheat Loaf (see
  pages 8 and 9)

pinch mixed dried herbs
salt and pepper
2 eggs, beaten
175 g/6 oz mixed nuts,
  finely chopped
cooking oil for deep
  frying

Cook the potatoes in lightly salted boiling water until
tender. Drain well and mash. Stir in the cheese and then the
breadcrumbs, herbs and seasoning. Leave to cool. Shape the
mixture into small balls and dip first in beaten egg and then
in the nuts to coat all over. Deep fry until golden brown.
Drain on kitchen paper and serve at once.

Coating for Deep-Fried Fish

100 g/4 oz rice crispies,
  finely ground
1 teaspoon dried dill
salt and pepper
1 large (size 1) egg,
  beaten

small squares of cod,
  strips of plaice or
  sole, or peeled
  prawns

Mix the rice crispies with the dill and seasoning. Dip the
chosen fish in the beaten egg and then coat in the rice crispy
mixture. Deep fry in hot cooking oil or shallow fry in plenty
of hot oil in a frying pan until crisp and golden. Drain on
kitchen paper and serve with wedges of lemon.

Cheesy Baked Cod

100 g/4 oz cornflakes,
   finely ground
50 g/2 oz Cheddar cheese,
   finely grated

salt and pepper
4 cod steaks
1 large (size 1) egg,
   beaten

Mix the cornflakes and cheese together and season. Cut the fish steaks into two or three pieces. Dip the pieces of fish into the beaten egg and then coat with the cornflake and cheese mixture. Place on a greased baking tray and bake at 190°C/ 375°F/Gas 5 for 15–20 minutes until the coating is crisp and the fish is cooked.

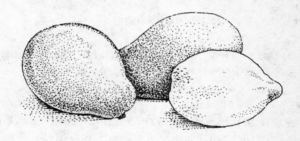

Fishcakes in a Cheese Coating

450 g/1 lb mashed
  potatoes
350 g/12 oz white fish,
  cooked and flaked, or
  2 × 200 g/7 oz cans
  tuna, trout or salmon,
  drained and flaked
salt and pepper

6 tablespoons flaked
  millet or flaked rice,
  ground in a food
  processor
3 tablespoons grated
  Parmesan cheese
cooking oil

Mix the potatoes and fish together with seasoning. Shape into flat cakes and leave to cool. Mix the ground flakes and cheese and use to coat the fishcakes. Shallow fry in oil.

Lamb Chops with a Nutty Coat

6 tablespoons rice
  crispies, crushed
3 tablespoons ground nuts

salt and pepper
4 lamb chops
1 egg, beaten

Mix the crushed rice crispies, ground nuts and seasoning in a bowl. Dip the lamb chops in egg and then in the rice crispy mixture, making sure that they are well coated. Place on a greased baking tray and bake at 190°C/375°F/Gas 5 for about 30–40 minutes until the chops are cooked. If you like your lamb well done cover with foil after 30 minutes and cook for about an hour.

Carolina Baked Chicken

For a change of flavour substitute 4–5 tablespoons toasted sesame seeds for the peanut butter and continue as directed below.

4 *chicken portions*
2 *eggs, beaten*
4 *tablespoons peanut butter, crunchy or smooth*

salt and pepper
4 *tablespoons cornflakes, crushed*

Skin the chicken joints and place on a greased baking tray. Beat the eggs with the peanut butter to form a paste. Season and spread over the chicken joints. Press on the cornflakes and bake at 190°C/375°F/Gas 5 for 45 minutes until the chicken is cooked and the coating is crisp.

Batters:

The Indians use a bean or pea based flour for many of their batters and this works very well. Yellow cornmeal, gluten-free cornflour and rice flour can also be pressed into service. See Sweet and Sour Pork on page 54 and Corn and Apple Pancake on page 29.

Light Batter for Tempura Fish and Vegetables

Cornflour gives a smoother effect than rice flour.

50 g/2 oz rice flour or   *50 ml/2 fl oz water*
   gluten-free cornflour   *2 egg whites*

Mix the rice flour or cornflour and water together to a smooth paste. Whisk the egg whites until stiff. Fold into flour mixture. Use to coat large peeled prawns, chunks of white fish such as cod or haddock, or very thinly sliced vegetables such as courgettes, carrots, swede or parsnips. Deep fry in hot cooking oil for 2–3 minutes until light and crisp. Drain on kitchen paper and serve at once.

Vegetable Pakoras   Makes 10–12 small pakoras

The batter for these tasty snacks is made from Baisan or
Channa flour (split pea flour). This can be bought at any
Indian or Chinese store and in some health food stores.
Serve as part of an Indian meal or as a cocktail canapé.

75 g/3 oz Baisan flour
½ teaspoon garam masala
   or curry powder
½ teaspoon salt
pepper
¼ teaspoon gluten-free
   baking powder
225 g/8 oz carrot,
   potato or parsnip,
   shredded, or a mixture
   of the three

1 tablespoon lemon juice
250–275 ml/8–9 fl oz
   water
cooking oil for deep
   frying

Mix all the dry ingredients together in a bowl. Stir in the
vegetables and then the lemon juice and sufficient water to
make a thick batter. Deep fry spoonfuls in hot fat for about
2–3 minutes until crisp and golden. Drain on kitchen paper.

Fried Onion Rings

75 g/3 oz Baisan, Channa
  or split pea flour
1/4 teaspoon ground cumin
salt and pepper
1 teaspoon lemon juice
250–275 ml/8–9 fl oz
  water

1 large onion or 2
  medium onions, cut
  into rings
cooking oil for deep
  frying

Cream the split pea flour, cumin and seasoning with the
lemon juice and sufficient water to make quite a thick
batter. Stir in the onion rings, making sure they are all well
coated. Drop into hot cooking oil and cook for about 2–3
minutes until crisp and golden. Drain on kitchen paper.

Corn Fritters

40 g/1 1/2 oz gluten-free
  cornflour or fine
  yellow cornmeal
15 g/1/2 oz rice flour
1/2 teaspoon gluten-free
  baking powder
1/4 teaspoon salt

1 egg, beaten
milk
100 g/4 oz frozen
  sweetcorn kernels,
  thawed
cooking oil for deep
  frying

Sift the dry ingredients into a bowl and beat in the egg and
sufficient milk to give a thick batter. Stir in the sweetcorn.
Drop spoonfuls of the mixture into hot fat and fry until
golden. Drain on kitchen paper and serve.

7

Sauces

Gluten-free cornflour can be used to thicken many sauces both savoury and sweet, but this flour does not have the consistency or flavour of sauces made with butter and wheatflour. Here are some alternative methods.

Basic Meat Gravy

Take the juices from the meat and add either extra meat stock or red wine and boil to concentrate the flavour. When the desired quantity is reached, colour with gluten-free gravy browning and thicken with half gluten-free cornflour and half potato flour. Mix the flours with a little cold water before adding to the stock and stir in away from the heat. If the mixture goes lumpy, sieve it. Heat through and serve.

Basic White Sauce

This can be made with a mixture of gluten-free cornflour and rice flour or gluten-free cornflour and potato flour or dried instant mashed potato powder. However, the latter mixture has a much more grainy texture. If you have time, infuse the milk with chopped onion and a bay leaf. This will give the sauce an even better flavour.

25 g/1 oz butter
15 g/½ oz gluten-free cornflour
15 g/½ oz rice flour or instant dried mashed potato powder

250–300 ml/8–10 fl oz milk
salt and pepper

Melt the butter in a saucepan and stir in the flours over a low heat. Pour in the milk and heat slowly, whisking with a wire balloon whisk until the mixture thickens and boils. If the mixture goes lumpy sieve it. Season and cook for 1 minute.

Cheese Sauce

Basic White Sauce
50–75 g/2–3 oz Cheddar cheese, grated

Stir in the cheese after the sauce has thickened and cook for 1 minute.

Parsley Sauce

Basic White Sauce
2–3 tablespoons freshly
  chopped parsley

Stir in the parsley just before serving the sauce.

Onion Sauce

Basic White Sauce
1 large onion, boiled
  and finely chopped

Stir in the onion after the sauce has thickened and cook for 1 minute.

Tomato- and vegetable-based sauces

Sauces can also be made simply by using the texture of vegetables cooked either in their own juices or in vegetable stock.

Tomato Sauce

1 onion, chopped
1 tablespoon cooking oil
1 × 400 g/14 oz can
   tomatoes
1 tablespoon tomato purée

½ teaspoon sugar
salt and pepper
basil, thyme, oregano
   or tarragon to flavour

Gently fry the onion in the cooking oil to soften it, then add all the remaining ingredients. Bring to the boil and simmer for 20 minutes. Purée in a blender or food processor and then rub through a sieve. Use the sauce as it is or thin it with vegetable stock or water and correct seasonings.

Other vegetable-based sauces are made in just the same way. 'Sweat' the chosen vegetables in a little butter and then add stock. Boil and purée.

Dairy sauces

Most of the dairy sauces using eggs, cream and butter given in general cookbooks will also be suitable for a gluten-free diet. Hollandaise, Béarnaise and mousseline sauces are good examples. They can be served with plainly grilled or fried meats and fish.

8

Pies, Tarts and Flans

Plain Shortcrust and Cheese Pastry

There are one or two quite good gluten-free pastry mixes on the market. However, you may find that they are better flavoured with sugar for dessert tarts and pastries or with herbs, nuts or cheese for savoury use. They may be used as bases for flans and tartlets or as toppings for pies. They may also be baked blind and used hot or cold for starters or cocktail canapés.

100 g/4 oz gluten-free
pastry mix

salt
2 tablespoons water

Optional flavourings:
2 tablespoons caster sugar
or
25 g/1 oz Cheddar cheese,
grated
or
½ teaspoon mixed dried
herbs

or
1 tablespoon flaked
almonds, toasted and
crushed

Mix the pastry mix with salt and water to form a good dough. Add a little more water if necessary. If using one of the flavourings, mix in with the water. Place on a lightly floured surface and roll out quite thinly. Use as directed in the recipe, or use to line 12 tartlet tins or an 18 cm/7 in flan tin. Bake blind at 200°C/400°F/Gas 6 until crisp and golden. Use hot or cold.

Potato Rice Pastry I

175 g/6 oz rice flour
175 g/6 oz maizemeal
    (fine) or gluten-free
    cornflour
1 teaspoon gluten-free
    baking powder

1/2 teaspoon salt
225 g/8 oz butter, cut
    into small pieces
175 g/6 oz mashed
    potatoes

Sift the flours into a bowl with the baking powder and salt. Add the butter and rub it into the flour until the mixure resembles fine breadcrumbs. Stir in the cold mashed potatoes and knead to a dough. Chill for 1 hour before use. Use as directed in the recipe, or roll out and use to line 8–10 tartlet tins. Bake blind at 200°C/400°F/Gas 6 for 15–20 minutes.

Potato Rice Pastry II

This recipe makes a very light and crisp pastry.

75 g/3 oz rice flour   salt
50 g/2 oz potato flour   75 g/3 oz butter
25 g/1 oz soya flour   1 egg, beaten

Mix the flours and salt in a bowl and add the butter cut into small pieces. Rub the butter into the flour until the mixture resembles fine breadcrumbs. Use sufficient egg to give a firm dough. Roll out on a floured surface and use as directed in the recipe, or use to line a flan tin or 10–12 tartlet cases. Bake blind at 200°C/400°F/Gas 6 for 10 minutes. Fill with scrambled egg or cottage cheese mixtures.

Blue Cheese Tartlets   Makes 16

15 g/½ oz gluten-free
  cornflour
15 g/½ oz rice flour
15 g/½ oz butter, melted
150 ml/¼ pint milk
75 g/3 oz blue cheese,
  cut into small pieces
100 g/4 oz quark or
  low-fat soft cheese

salt and pepper
4–6 spring onions,
  finely chopped
12 plain shortcrust
  tartlets, baked blind
  (see page 81)

Mix the cornflour, rice flour, melted butter and a little milk
to a smooth paste. Stir in the rest of the milk and place in a
heavy-based pan. Bring to the boil, stirring all the time. Stir
in the blue cheese, quark and seasoning. Leave to cool. Stir
in the spring onions and use to fill the tartlets.

Ham and Egg Tartlets

This recipe can be made with plain shortcrust or cheese pastry but the latter is particularly good. It can also be made in a large flan tin.

Plain Shortcrust or Cheese Pastry (see page 81)
1 egg, beaten
150 ml/¼ pint single cream
50 g/2 oz cooked ham, diced
2 tablespoons frozen peas, thawed
salt and pepper
pinch mixed herbs

Roll out the pastry and use to line 12 tartlet cases. Mix all the remaining ingredients and spoon into the tartlet cases. Bake at 200°C/400°F/Gas 6 for 12 minutes until the tarts are set in the centre and lightly browned. A larger flan will take a little longer to cook.

Mixed Vegetable Quiche

½ quantity Potato Rice
  Pastry I or II (see
  pages 82 and 83)
1 small onion, sliced
½ green pepper, seeded
  and sliced
25 g/1 oz butter
1 tablespoon cooking
  oil
100 g/4 oz button
  mushrooms, sliced

50 g/2 oz Cheddar
  cheese, grated
2 eggs, beaten
150 ml/¼ pint single
  cream
salt and pepper
a little milk
2 courgettes, sliced

Roll out the pastry and use to line a 20 cm/8 in loose-based flan tin. Gently fry the onion and pepper in the butter and oil for 2–3 minutes. Add the mushrooms and continue to fry over a low heat for 5 minutes to soften all the vegetables. Spread over the bottom of the flan case and cover with the cheese. Beat the eggs with the cream, seasoning and sufficient milk to fill the flan. Pour over the cheese and vegetables. Add a little more milk if necessary, stirring it in with a fork. Arrange the sliced courgettes round the top of the flan. Bake at 190°C/375°F/Gas 5 for 35–40 minutes until the quiche is set in the centre and the top is lightly browned.

Tomato Cheese Flan

75 g/3 oz cornflakes,
    finely ground
25 g/1 oz walnuts,
    finely ground
75 g/3 oz butter,
    melted
1 teaspoon tomato purée
salt and pepper
225 g/8 oz quark or
    low-fat soft cheese

50 g/2 oz Cheddar
    cheese, grated
1 sweet-sour pickled
    cucumber, finely
    chopped
1 tablespoon freshly
    chopped parsley
4 tomatoes, skinned
    and sliced
sprigs of parsley

Mix the cornflakes, walnuts, butter, tomato purée and seasoning and pile the mixture into a 20 cm/8 in flan tin. Press well down with your fingers. Place in the refrigerator to set. After about 1 hour, mix the cheeses, cucumber and parsley and season to taste. Spread the mixture over the set base. Decorate the top with slices of tomato and sprigs of parsley.

Curried Egg Flan

25 g/1 oz cornflakes,
  finely ground
50 g/2 oz rice crispies,
  finely ground
25 g/1 oz mixed nuts,
  finely ground
1/2 teaspoon curry powder

1/4 teaspoon ground cumin
75 g/3 oz butter, melted,
  plus butter for
  cooking the eggs
5 eggs, beaten
salt and pepper
75 g/3 oz peas, cooked

Mix together the cornflakes, rice crispies and nuts and stir in the spices. Pour on the melted butter and mix thoroughly. Pile into a 20 cm/8 in flan ring. Press down well with your fingers. Place in the refrigerator to chill and set. Meanwhile, scramble the eggs in a little butter. Season to taste and leave to cool. Spoon over the set base, remove from the flan ring and decorate the top with a ring of cooked peas round the edge. Serve at once.

Watercress and Rice Flan

225 g/8 oz long-grain
   rice
450 ml/³/4 pint water
salt and pepper
2 carrots, cooked and
   sieved
150 ml/¹/4 pint soured
   cream
1 bunch watercress,
   washed and chopped
   with a few sprigs
   left whole

3 tablespoons quark or
   low-fat soft cheese
1 hard-boiled egg,
   sliced
2–3 tomatoes, skinned
   and sliced

Put the rice, water and salt into a pan and bring to the boil. Stir once, cover with a lid and reduce the heat. Cook for 12–15 minutes until the rice is tender and all the liquid has been absorbed. Cool a little, then mix in the carrot, soured cream and seasoning. Spoon into the bottom of a 20 cm/8 in flan tin and press well down. Leave to cool, then chill for 1 hour. Mix the chopped watercress with the quark and spread over the chilled rice base. Remove from the flan tin then decorate the top with sliced hard-boiled egg, sliced tomato and the retained sprigs of watercress. Serve at once.

Bakewell Tart

½ quantity Potato Rice
  Pastry I or II (see
  pages 82 and 83)
50 g/2 oz raspberry jam
4 eggs

100 g/4 oz sugar
100 g/4 oz butter
100 g/4 oz ground
  almonds

Roll out the pastry and use to line a 20 cm/8 in flan tin, or use individual tartlet tins. Cover the bottom of the pastry case with jam. Beat the eggs and sugar until pale and thick. Melt the butter and gradually pour onto the egg mixture, stirring all the time. Fold in the almonds and spoon into the pastry case. Bake at 200°C/400°F/Gas 6 for about 35–40 minutes until the filling is set. Serve warm or cold with cream or custard.

Fruit pies

Potato rice pastry II is particularly suited to this kind of application. It makes a very light crumbly topping for fruit pies.

900 g/2 lb stewed fruit
  (gooseberries,
  blackberry and apple,
  plums or greengages)

sugar to taste
Potato Rice Pastry II
  (see page 83)

Place the fruit in the bottom of a pie dish and add sugar to taste. Roll out the pastry and place on the top of the pie. Flute the edges and prick the top well with a fork. Bake at 200°C/400°F/Gas 6 for 12–15 minutes until crisp and golden.

Jam Tarts

Potato Rice Pastry II
  (see page 83)
4–5 tablespoons jam
  or lemon curd

milk

Roll out the pastry and use to line 10–12 tartlet tins. Place a teaspoonful of jam in the bottom of each tart case. Do not overfill or the jam may boil over. Brush the pastry rims with a little milk and bake at 190°C/375°F/Gas 5 for about 15–20 minutes. Check that the bases of the tarts are cooked through. Transfer to a wire rack to cool.

Coconut and Pecan Flan Case

50 g/2 oz cornflakes,
  finely ground
25 g/1 oz desiccated
  coconut

25 g/1 oz pecan nuts,
  finely ground
75 g/3 oz melted butter

Mix all the ingredients together and pile into a 20 cm/8 in flan ring. Press down very well with your fingers and chill until set.

Suggested toppings:
A mixture of soft fruits including raspberries, sliced straw-
  berries and blackcurrants
Sliced fresh pears topped with a glaze of raspberry jam
Apple Purée flavoured with raisins and a pinch of cinnamon

Pineapple Ginger Flan

This coconut mixture makes an excellent base for any kind of cold flan or for uncooked cheesecake.

Base:
25 g/1 oz rice crispies
25 g/1 oz desiccated
  coconut
75 g/3 oz butter
25 g/1 oz sugar

Topping:
Ginger marmalade
1 can crushed pineapple,
  well drained
100 g/4 oz quark or
  low-fat soft cheese
150 ml/¼ pint double
  cream, whipped
pieces of crystallized
  ginger, finely chopped

Crush the rice crispies and mix with the coconut. Melt the butter and sugar in a saucepan and stir over a low heat until the sugar has dissolved. Pour over the dry ingredients and press into an 8 in/20 cm loose-based flan tin. Chill until set. Remove the base from the flan tin and spread with ginger marmalade. Mix all the remaining ingredients and pile onto the base. Keep in the fridge until required.

Orange Cheesecake Flan

50 g/2 oz cornflakes,
   finely ground
25 g/1 oz ground almonds
75 g/3 oz butter, melted
25 g/1 oz sugar
3 oranges
225 g/8 oz cottage
   cheese

75 g/3 oz quark or
   low-fat soft cheese
150 ml/¼ pint orange
   juice
15 g/¼ oz gelatine

Mix together the ground cornflakes, almonds, butter and sugar and pile into a 20 cm/8 in flan tin. Press well down with your fingers and place in the refrigerator to set. Meanwhile, grate a little orange rind into a blender or food processor. Peel the oranges and add the chopped flesh to the rind. Next add the cheeses, and most of the orange juice. Blend to a smooth cream. Dissolve the gelatine in the remaining orange juice. Mix into the orange cream. Pour the mixture over the set flan base and return to the refrigerator. Chill for 2 hours and serve.

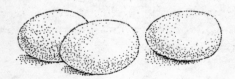

9

Puddings

Jam or Marmalade Pudding

Steamed puddings can be made very successfully with gluten-free flour.

175 g/6 oz gluten-free
   self-raising flour,
   sifted (Trufree No 7)
100 g/4 oz butter
100 g/4 oz sugar

pinch salt
2 eggs, beaten
2–3 tablespoons milk
175 g/6 oz jam or
   marmalade

Place the flour in a bowl and add the butter cut into small pieces. Rub the butter into the flour until the mixture resembles breadcrumbs and then stir in the sugar and salt. Mix to a dropping consistency with eggs and milk. Line a 1.5 litre/2½ pint buttered pudding basin with jam or marmalade and spoon in the mixture. Cover with greaseproof paper and steam for 1½–2 hours. Turn out and serve with melted jam or marmalade.

'Chocolate' Steamed Pudding

This mixture makes an excellent sponge pudding. Use dried fruit, chopped ginger or marmalade in place of the carob powder as desired and fold in at the end.

75 g/3 oz gluten-free cornflour	*100 g/4 oz butter*
25 g/1 oz rice flour	*100 g/4 oz sugar*
25 g/1 oz soya flour	*pinch salt*
15 g/½ oz carob powder	*2 eggs, beaten*
1 teaspoon gluten-free baking powder	*2–3 tablespoons milk*

Place the three flours, carob powder and baking powder in a bowl and add the butter cut into small pieces. Rub the fat into the flour until the mixture resembles breadcrumbs and stir in the sugar and salt. Mix to a dropping consistency with the eggs and milk. Spoon into a buttered 1 litre/1½ pint pudding basin. Cover with greaseproof paper and steam for 1½–2 hours. Turn out and serve with custard.

Homemade Bread and Butter Pudding

Either the White Bread recipe (page 7) or bought gluten-free bread will make the nearest to white bread and butter pudding. However, the other recipes in Chapter 1 can also be pressed into service. This recipe is a useful way of using up any stale bread.

4–6 slices White Bread (see page 7)	2 tablespoons sugar
	1 egg, beaten
butter	150 ml/¼ pint milk
1 tablespoon raisins	pinch grated nutmeg

Butter the bread and cut off some of the crusts. Arrange the bread in layers in a well-greased pie dish. Sprinkle raisins and sugar between the layers of bread. Beat the egg and milk and pour over the top. Sprinkle with nutmeg and a little more sugar and leave to stand for 15 minutes. Bake at 180°C/350°F/Gas 4 for 30 minutes until the centre is set and the top is golden in colour.

Fruit Crumble

This crumble is almost indistinguishable from that made with wheatflour.

100 g/4 oz gluten-free
   cornflour
75 g/3 oz rice flour
75 g/3 oz butter or
   margarine

75 g/3 oz sugar
25 g/1 oz nuts, chopped
700 g/1½ lb stewed
   apples or other fruit

Sift together the flours and rub in the butter or margarine until the mixture resembles breadcrumbs. Stir in the sugar and nuts. Place the fruit in an ovenproof dish and cover with the crumble. Bake at 200°C/400°F/Gas 6 for 25–30 minutes until golden brown.

Sweet Potato Pudding

This makes a deliciously light and fluffy baked pudding.
Serve in place of steamed or baked puddings made with
wheatflour.

75 ml/3 fl oz hot water
*100 g/4 oz desiccated
coconut*
*450 g/1 lb sweet
potatoes*
*75 g/3 oz soft brown
sugar*
25 g/1 oz butter
2 eggs, beaten

grated lemon rind
1 tablespoon lemon juice
*½ teaspoon gluten-free
baking powder*
*¼ teaspoon ground
cinnamon*
salt
*2 tablespoons Barbados
sugar*

Pour the water over the coconut and leave to soak. Bake the
sweet potatoes at 190°C/375°F/Gas 5 for 1–1½ hours until
tender all the way through. Scrape the potato flesh out of the
skins and mash well. Stir in the butter and brown sugar and
beat until well mixed in. Stir in all the remaining ingredients
except the Barbados sugar. Drain the liquid off the coconut
and stir into the potato mixture. Spoon into a soufflé dish
and top with the Barbados sugar. Bake at 190°C/375°F/Gas
5 for 20 minutes. Reduce the heat to 100°C/325°F/Gas 2
and continue baking until the pudding is well risen and the
sugar topping is brown. Serve hot.

Baked Fruit Pudding

Soft fruit can be cooked under the sponge topping. Harder fruits may need to be lightly cooked first.

700 g/1½ lb stewed fruit

Topping:
100 g/4 oz sugar
100 g/4 oz butter
2 eggs, beaten
75 g/3 oz gluten-free cornflour
25 g/1 oz rice flour

25 g/1 oz ground almonds
1 tablespoon dried milk powder
pinch salt

Place the fruit in the bottom of a pie dish. To make the topping, cream the butter with the sugar until light and fluffy. Beat in the eggs one at a time, adding a little cornflour at the same time. Stir in the remaining cornflour, the rice flour, almonds, milk powder and salt. Spoon over the fruit and bake at 180°C/350°F/Gas 4 for 1¼ hours. Cover with foil after 45 minutes. Eat hot.

Apple Charlotte

Raisin bread made with gluten-free flour is particularly good in this recipe, but any of the other plain breads could be used.

175 g/6 oz stale
   gluten-free bread
   made into breadcrumbs
50–75 g/2–3 oz butter
700 g/1½ lb cooking
   apples, peeled, cored
   and sliced

sugar to taste
pinch ground cinnamon

Fry the breadcrumbs in the butter until crisp and golden. Layer the sliced apples and breadcrumbs in a pie dish, sprinkling with a little sugar and cinnamon as you go. Finish with a layer of breadcrumbs. Dot with a little more butter and bake at 200°C/400°F/Gas 6 for 20–30 minutes until the apples are cooked through.

Hot Lemon Rice Soufflé

100 g/4 oz pudding rice	*4 eggs, separated*
600 ml/1 pint milk	*grated rind of 1 large*
175 g/6 oz butter	*or 2 small lemons*
175 g/6 oz sugar	*lemon curd to serve*

Place the rice, milk, butter and sugar in the top of a double saucepan. Pour about 7.5 cm/3 in water into the bottom half and bring to the boil. Reduce the heat and cover the top half with a lid. Simmer for 1½–2 hours or until thick and creamy. Leave to cool. Mix in the egg yolks and the lemon rind. Whisk the egg whites until they are very stiff and fold into the rice mixture. Spoon into a buttered soufflé dish and bake at 180°C/350°F/Gas 4 for about 1 hour or until lightly browned on the top and set in the centre. Serve at once, with a spoonful of lemon curd on each portion.

Lemon Pancakes
Makes 8–10

Eat at once—these pancakes will not keep.

150 g/6 oz gluten-free cornflour
pinch of salt
2 eggs
300 ml/½ pint milk

2 tablespoons pure corn oil
sugar and lemon juice to serve

Sift the cornflour and salt into a bowl. Make a well in the centre and add the eggs and half the milk. Beat until smooth, and stir in the remainder of the milk. Heat a little corn oil in a frying pan and pour in sufficient batter to cover the pan thinly. Cook until golden brown. Toss the pancake or turn with a knife and cook the other side. Turn onto a plate, sprinkle with a little sugar and lemon juice and roll up.

'Chocolate' Cherry Pots   Serves 4–6

This easy-to-make family dessert is certainly good enough for entertaining. Add a little sherry and top with whipped cream and more nuts and cherries for a festive effect.

40 g/1½ oz gluten-free
    cornflour
25 g/1 oz carob powder
50 g/2 oz sugar
1 egg, separated

600 ml/1 pint milk
25 g/1 oz glacé
    cherries, chopped
25 g/1 oz nuts, finely
    chopped

Blend the cornflour, carob powder and sugar with the egg yolk and 3–4 tablespoons milk. Heat the remaining milk in a pan and pour over the cornflour and carob mixture, stirring all the time. Return to the pan and bring to the boil, stirring all the time. Simmer for 1–2 minutes. Remove from the heat and stir in the cherries and nuts. Whisk the egg white until very stiff. Stir a spoonful into the mixture and carefully fold in the rest. Spoon into a large glass bowl or into individual glass dishes and leave to cool. Chill for 1 hour before serving.

Pear and Ginger Trifle

This trifle is a real party-stopper; everyone will come rushing back for more.

½ gluten-free Ginger-
   bread (see page 117)
1 × 400 g/14 oz can
   pears in pear juice
3 tablespoons ginger
   wine

1 × 425 g/15 oz can
   Devon Cream Custard
150 ml/¼ pint double
   cream, whipped
hundreds and thousands

Slice the cake and the pears, retaining the pear juice. Layer the cake and fruit in a bowl. Pour on the pear juice and the ginger wine. Cover with the custard and top with the cream. Chill for at least 1 hour. Decorate with hundreds and thousands just before serving.

Creamed Carob Whip

15 g/½ oz cornflour
15 g/½ oz carob powder
3 tablespoons sugar
1 egg, beaten
200 ml/7½ fl oz milk

150 ml/¼ pint double
cream, whipped
25 g/1 oz mixed nuts,
chopped

Mix the cornflour, carob powder and sugar in a bowl with the egg and 3–4 tablespoons cold milk. Heat the remaining milk in a saucepan. Bring almost to the boil and pour over the cornflour and carob mixture, stirring all the time. Return to the pan and bring to the boil, stirring all the time. Boil for 1 minute, then leave to cool with a piece of baking parchment paper covering the surface. Mix the whipped cream into the carob mixture. Mix in half the nuts. Spoon into individual bowls and top with the rest of the nuts. Chill until required.

Indian Rice Balls

300 ml/1½ pints milk
50 g/2 oz pudding rice
1 stick cinnamon
50 g/2 oz caster sugar
1 tablespoon raisins

desiccated coconut
extra sugar to serve
cream or thick plain
*   yogurt*

Place the milk, rice, cinnamon, sugar and raisins in the top part of a double saucepan. Pour about 7.5 cm/3 in water into the base and bring to the boil. Reduce the heat, cover the top half with a lid and simmer for 1¾ hours, stirring from time to time. The mixture should be thick. Discard the cinnamon stick. Leave to cool and chill. Just before serving, shape the mixture into balls and roll in coconut. Serve with sugar and cream or thick yogurt.

Cakes, Buns and Biscuits

Date and Cherry Crispy Fingers   Makes about 16

*100 g/4 oz butter or
    margarine*
50 g/2 oz brown sugar
*225 g/8 oz stoned dates,
    chopped*
*10 glacé cherries,
    chopped*

75 g/3 oz rice crispies
*25 g/1 oz nuts, chopped
    (hazelnuts, almonds
    or Brazils)*
*2 × 65 g/2½ oz blocks
    sweetened carob,
    melted*

Place the butter or margarine in a saucepan with the sugar,
dates and cherries and cook over a low heat for about 5
minutes until the sugar has dissolved and the fruit is soft.
Place the rice crispies in a bowl and pour on the date
mixture. Mix thoroughly, if necessary using your hands
after they have been dipped in cold water. Press the mixture
into a tin about 23 × 15 cm/9 × 6 in and top with the melted
carob block. Leave in a cool place to set. Cut into fingers to
serve.

Lemon Biscuits   Makes 15

For special occasions stick pairs of biscuits together with
lemon curd and dredge with icing sugar. Or flavour with
grated orange rind for a change.

100 g/4 oz butter or   *1 egg, beaten*
    margarine   *225 g/8 oz gluten-free*
100 g/4 oz caster sugar   *cornflour*
grated rind of 1 lemon

Beat the butter or margarine, sugar and lemon rind together
until light and creamy. Beat in the egg and then the cornflour. Turn the mixture onto a floured board and knead
lightly. Roll out thinly and cut into 15 biscuits. Place on a
baking tray lined with greased greaseproof paper or baking
parchment paper. Bake at 180°C/350°F/Gas 4 for 20
minutes until light golden in colour.

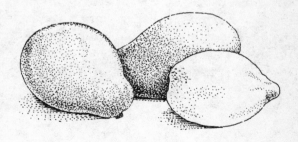

Apple and Nut Cookies   Makes 8

50 g/2 oz butter or
  margarine
100 g/4 oz ground rice
75 g/3 oz eating apple,
  peeled and finely
  grated
25 g/1 oz nuts, finely
  chopped

25 g/1 oz raisins,
  chopped
1 tablespoon soft brown
  sugar
1/4 teaspoon mixed spice

Cut the butter or margarine into the ground rice and mix
with a fork. Add the apple, nuts, raisins, sugar and spice and
mix with a wooden spoon until a large ball of dough has
formed. Roll out the dough to 5 mm/1/4 in thick and cut into
8 biscuits with a pastry cutter. Place on a baking tray. Bake
at 230°C/450°F/Gas 8 for about 10–12 minutes and remove
to a wire rack with a spatula. The cookies will go crisp as
they cool.

Peanut Fingers   Makes 8–10

Almonds or hazelnuts can be used in place of peanuts in this recipe.

50 g/2 oz peanuts,   *75 g/3 oz caster sugar*
  finely ground   *1 egg white*
15 g/½ oz ground rice   *rice paper*
  or medium cornmeal

Mix the peanuts with the ground rice or cornmeal and the sugar. Whisk the egg white until very stiff. Stir a spoonful into the mixture and fold in the rest. Spoon short lengths onto a baking tray lined with rice paper or baking parchment paper. Bake at 160°C/325°F/Gas 3 for 15 minutes until the biscuits begin to turn golden in colour. Cool for 2–3 minutes and then transfer to a wire rack to cool completely.

Coconut Mountains   Makes 8

1 egg white   *100 g/4 oz desiccated*
1 teaspoon lemon juice   *coconut*
100 g/4 oz caster sugar   *rice paper*

Whisk the egg white until very stiff. Fold in the lemon juice and sugar and whisk again until stiff. Stir in the coconut. Place spoonfuls on a baking tray lined with rice paper. Bake at 160°C/325°F/Gas 3 for about 20 minutes, until the coconut mountains are just beginning to turn golden in colour.

Carob Date Fingers   Makes about 16

For special occasions coat these fingers with melted carob blocks. If you cannot find rice cakes use about 100–125 g/4–5 oz rice crispies instead.

100 g/4 oz margarine
   or butter
100 g/4 oz caster sugar
225 g/8 oz stoned dates,
   chopped
2 level tablespoons
   carob powder

1 egg, beaten
50 g/2 oz desiccated
   coconut
1 packet gluten-free
   puffed rice cakes,
   crushed

Melt the margarine or butter in a pan and add the sugar and dates. Cook for about 5 minutes until the dates are soft and the sugar has dissolved. Blend in the carob powder and remove from the heat. Cool before adding the egg. Mix well and stir in the coconut and crushed rice cakes. Spread in a Swiss roll tin and leave in a cool place to set. Cut into fingers to serve.

Ginger Millet Flapjack
Makes about 16 squares

This mixture makes an excellent flapjack without using rolled oats.

100 g/4 oz flaked
   millet
50 g/2 oz flaked rice
50 g/2 oz rice flour
1 teaspoon ground ginger

pinch salt
100 g/4 oz butter
75 g/3 oz sugar
2 tablespoons golden
   syrup

Place the dry ingredients in a bowl. Gently warm together the butter, sugar and syrup and stir into the dry ingredients. Mix well and press into a shallow 20 cm/8 in square tin lined with baking parchment paper. Bake at 160°C/325°F/Gas 3 for 15–20 minutes until golden brown. Leave to cool for a few minutes before cutting into squares. Leave to cool in the tin.

Syrup Crispies

Makes 8

For an unusual variation on this recipe use honey in place of syrup and add 1 teaspoon grated orange rind.

25 g/1 oz rice crispies
15 g/½ oz butter or
  margarine

25 g/1 oz sugar
2 teaspoons golden
  syrup

Put the rice crispies in a warmed bowl. Mix all the remaining ingredients in a pan and bring to the boil. Simmer for 4–5 minutes and pour over the rice crispies. Mix very quickly together and drop spoonfuls onto waxed paper or into paper bun cases. Leave to set.

Rice and Nut Clusters

Makes 12

These crispy clusters are also very good made with lightly crushed cornflakes.

50 g/2 oz block carob,
   cut into pieces
25 g/1 oz butter
1 tablespoon syrup
1 tablespoon brown
   sugar

25 g/1 oz nuts, chopped
   (almonds, hazelnuts,
   walnuts)
25 g/1 oz raisins,
   chopped
25 g/1 oz rice crispies

Melt the carob in a basin over a pan of hot water. Melt the butter in a saucepan and stir in the syrup and sugar. Bring to the boil and simmer for 3–4 minutes. Stir in the melted carob and then stir in the nuts, raisins and rice crispies until the mixture forms a fairly stiff cluster. Try not to stir too much or the rice crispies will be crushed. Place spoonfuls in rough clusters on waxed paper or in paper bun cases and leave in a cool place to harden.

Melting Moments   Makes 12–14

These very light biscuits need great care in handling when removing from the baking tray. Transfer at once to a wire rack using a fish slice to lift each one in one piece.

100 g/4 oz butter or
  margarine
75 g/3 oz sugar
1 small egg, beaten
1 teaspoon vanilla
  essence
125 g/5 oz gluten-free
  cornflour, sifted

1 level teaspoon
  gluten-free baking
  powder
1 small (25 g/1 oz) box
  cornflakes, crushed

Cream the butter or margarine and sugar together until light and fluffy. Add the beaten egg and vanilla essence and stir in the cornflour and baking powder. Drop teaspoonfuls of the mixture into the crushed cornflakes and roll to coat evenly. Place on a very well-greased baking tray and bake at 190°C/375°F/Gas 5 for 15–18 minutes until golden brown. Carefully transfer to a wire rack to cool.

Gingerbread

Makes 20 squares

100 g/4 oz margarine
175 g/6 oz black
  treacle
50 g/2 oz golden syrup
150 ml/¼ pint milk
2 eggs, beaten
225 g/8 oz gluten-free
  flour

1 teaspoon mixed spice
1 tablespoon ground
  ginger
1 teaspoon bicarbonate
  of soda
50 g/2 oz caster sugar

Combine the margarine, treacle and syrup in a saucepan and heat but do not boil. Add the milk. Leave to cool and beat in the eggs. Sift together the flour, spices and bicarbonate of soda and mix in the sugar. Make a well in the dry ingredients and pour in the liquid. Mix together to form a smooth batter. Pour into a greased and lined 18 cm/7 in square cake tin and bake at 150°C/300°F/Gas 2 for 1¼ hours. Leave to cool in the tin for 10 minutes before turning out onto a wire rack to cool completely.

Rice and Raisin Buns   Makes 12

These buns are very good plain or iced with vanilla or lemon water icing.

100 g/4 oz rice flour
100 g/4 oz gluten-free
   cornflour
2 level teaspoons
   gluten-free baking
   powder
50 g/2 oz butter or
   margarine

25 g/1 oz sugar
50 g/2 oz raisins,
   chopped
1 egg
75 ml/3 fl oz milk

Sift together the rice flour, cornflour and baking powder and rub in the butter or margarine. Add the sugar, raisins, egg and milk. Drop spoonfuls into well-greased bun tins or into paper bun cases. Place the bun cases on a baking tray and bake at 190°C/375°F/Gas 5 for about 12–15 minutes until cooked through and golden brown on top. Transfer buns from the bun tins to a wire rack to cool.

Date and Walnut Loaf

This excellent tea loaf is as good as any made with wheatflour. Take care in turning it out as it may be a little crumbly when hot.

100 g/4 oz rice flour
50 g/2 oz maizemeal
50 g/2 oz polenta or yellow cornmeal
1 level teaspoon gluten-free baking powder
1 level teaspoon bicarbonate of soda
100 g/4 oz soft brown sugar

150 g/6 oz stoned cooking dates, chopped
50 g/2 oz walnuts, chopped
4 tablespoons corn oil
1 egg
6 tablespoons milk

Sift together the various flours, baking powder and bicarbonate of soda and stir in the sugar, dates and walnuts. Mix together the corn oil, egg and milk and add to the dry ingredients to give a soft dropping consistency. Turn into a 450 g/1 lb loaf tin that has been oiled and lined with baking parchment paper. Bake at 180°C/350°F/Gas 4 for 50 minutes to an hour. Turn out and cool on a wire rack.

Cream and Jam Sponge Sandwich

This mixture will also make 24 fairy cakes.

3 eggs, separated
100 g/4 oz caster
  sugar
75 g/3 oz gluten-free
  cornflour

3 tablespoons raspberry
  or strawberry jam
75 ml/3 fl oz double
  cream, whipped
icing sugar

Whisk the egg whites until stiff. Add the yolks and continue beating. Add the sugar and beat until the mixture leaves a trail. Fold in the cornflour and turn into 2 greased 20 cm/ 8 in sandwich tins. Bake at 190°C/375°F/Gas 5 for 20–25 minutes until golden brown. Cool on a wire rack. Sandwich together with jam and cream and dust the top with icing sugar before serving.

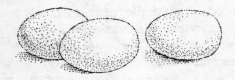

Lemon Curd Cake

Decorate with lemon-flavoured water icing for a change. In this instance omit the jam from the top of the cake.

100 g/4 oz butter
100 g/4 oz sugar
grated rind of 1 lemon
2 eggs, beaten
6 tablespoons lemon curd
100 g/4 oz gluten-free cornflour, or 75 g/3 oz gluten-free cornflour mixed with 25 g/1 oz potato flour

2 tablespoons rice flour
1 teaspoon gluten-free baking powder

Cream the butter, sugar and grated lemon rind until light and creamy. Gradually beat in the eggs and stir in 1 tablespoon of lemon curd. Sift the flours and baking powder together and fold into the mixture. Turn into a greased and lined 15 cm/6 in cake tin. Bake at 180°C/350°F/Gas 4 for 50 minutes to 1 hour until golden brown and risen. Brush the top of the cake with 2 tablespoons of lemon curd while it is still hot. When the cake is cold, remove from the tin and slice through the centre. Fill with the remaining lemon curd.

Sweet Potato Cake

450 g/1 lb sweet
    potatoes
25 g/1 oz butter
50 g/2 oz gluten-free
    cornflour
50 g/2 oz coarse
    cornmeal or polenta
75 g/3 oz Muscovado
    sugar

2 eggs, beaten
2 tablespoons milk
grated rind of 1 lemon
1 heaped teaspoon
    gluten-free baking
    powder
pinch ground allspice
pinch salt

Bake the sweet potatoes at 200°C/400°F/Gas 6 for 1–1½ hours until soft. Reduce the heat to 180°C/350°F/Gas 4. Peel and mash the potatoes and beat in all the other ingredients. Pour into a 450 g/1 lb loaf tin that has been lined with baking parchment paper and bake for 1 hour until a skewer comes out clean. Cool and turn out onto a wire rack. Cut into slices to serve.

Almond Cake

This cake can also be made with ground hazelnuts in place of the almonds. Use 325 g/11 oz in total.

300 g/10 oz ground
   almonds
25 g/1 oz ground
   hazelnuts
25 g/1 oz gluten-free
   puffed rice cakes,
   ground

225 g/8 oz demerara
   sugar
6 eggs, separated

Mix the dry ingredients with the egg yolks. Whisk the egg whites until stiff and fold into the mixture. Line the bottom of a 15 cm/6 in cake tin with baking parchment paper and spoon in the mixture. Bake at 180°C/350°F/Gas 4 for 1 hour, then turn the oven up to 200°C/400°F/Gas 6 and bake for a further 15 minutes. Cover with foil at this stage if the cake shows signs of getting too brown.

Lemon Rice Cake

*175 g/6 oz butter or
   margarine*
150 g/5 oz sugar
2 eggs
*150 g/5 oz gluten-free
   self-raising flour, or
   gluten-free flour plus
   1 teaspoon gluten-free
   baking powder*

*75 g/3 oz ground rice
grated rind of 1 lemon
lemon water icing*

Cream the butter or margarine and sugar until light and fluffy. Add one egg and a little flour and beat well. Add the second egg and some more flour. Beat again. Fold in the remaining flour, the ground rice and lemon rind. Spoon into a 450 g/1 lb loaf tin and bake at 190°C/375°F/Gas 5 for about 1 hour until lightly browned and firm to the touch. Leave to cool and then drizzle with lemon water icing.

Fruit Cake

100 g/4 oz rice flour
25 g/1 oz soya flour
75 g/3 oz gluten-free
  cornflour
40 g/1 ½ oz ground
  almonds
2 level teaspoons
  gluten-free baking
  powder
1 level teaspoon mixed
  spice

75 g/3 oz margarine
100 g/4 oz soft brown
  sugar
225 g/8 oz dried mixed
  fruit
25 g/1 oz walnuts,
  chopped
50 g/2 oz glacé cherries
3 eggs, lightly beaten
2 tablespoons milk

Sift together the flours, almonds, baking powder and spice and rub in the margarine until the mixture resembles breadcrumbs. Add the sugar, mixed fruit, walnuts and cherries. Stir in the eggs and milk to form a soft dropping consistency. Turn into a greased and lined 18 cm/7 in round cake tin. Bake at 180°C/350°F/Gas 4 for 1 hour. Leave to cool in the tin and then turn onto a wire rack.

Potato Fruit Cake

450 g/1 lb potatoes,
  cooked
100 g/4 oz icing sugar
50 g/2 oz glacé cherries
25 g/1 oz seedless
  raisins
25 g/1 oz chopped
  candied peel

50 g/2 oz butter, melted
few drops of vanilla
  essence
2 eggs, separated
caster or icing sugar
  to dredge

Take care not to overcook the potatoes. Drain them well
and leave to cool. Sieve the potatoes into a basin and mix
with the sugar, cherries, raisins, peel, butter and vanilla
essence. Beat in the egg yolks. Whisk the whites until they
are really stiff and stir a couple of tablespoons into the
potato mixture. Fold in the rest of the egg whites. Spoon
into a greased 20 cm/8 in cake tin and bake at 190°C/375°F/
Gas 5 for 40–45 minutes until lightly browned and set in the
centre. Turn out onto a wire rack to cool. Sprinkle with
sugar to serve.

Refrigerator Cake

100 g/4 oz block carob
1 egg
25 g/1 oz sugar
1 teaspoon instant
    coffee powder
few drops of vanilla
    essence
100 g/4 oz butter,
    melted

100 g/4 oz cold mashed
    potatoes
100 g/4 oz cake crumbs
    (use Gingerbread,
    page 117, or Date and
    Walnut Loaf, page 119)

Melt the carob in a basin over a pan of hot water. Beat the egg and sugar together with the instant coffee and vanilla essence. Beat in the butter and then the melted carob. Finally fold in the potatoes and the crumbs.

Line a 450 g/1 lb loaf tin with baking parchment paper and press the cake mixture into the tin. Chill in the refrigerator for at least 2 hours. Turn out and cut into slices. Serve with fresh cream or yogurt.

Appendix

Special foods and where to find them

The following list is taken from my own experience with gluten-free cooking. There may be other products which are just as good. They are available from supermarkets, some chemists or from health food shops.

GLUTEN-FREE FLOURS
Brown and Polson Cornflour from any supermarket
Yeoman Instant Mashed Potato from any supermarket
Trufree Flours Range 1–7, also by direct mail from The Cantassium Company, Larkhill Laboratories, 225–229 Putney Bridge, London SW15 2PY
Juvela Low Protein Mix

GLUTEN-FREE PASTRY MIX
G.F. Brand (manufactured in Sweden). Information from G.F. Dietary Supplies Ltd, Lowther Road, Stanmore, Middlesex

FLAKES
Zwicky Soya bean flakes
Zwicky millet flakes
Hofels millet and rice flakes
Holland and Barratt own-label rice and millet flakes

BISCUITS
G.F. Brand Muesli Fruit Biscuits
G.F. Brand Gluten Free Crackers
G.F. Brand thin wafer bread
Edward and Sons Baked Brown Rice Snaps
La Source de Vie Puffed Rice Cakes

MISCELLANEOUS PRODUCTS TO LOOK OUT FOR
Carob powder for use in place of cocoa
Rice or soya bran for use in place of wheat bran
Gluten-free baking powder

For information on everyday manufactured products which are gluten-free, contact the Coeliac Society, PO Box 181, London NW2 2QY. This organisation publishes a very comprehensive list of products. The list is available at a modest fee.

Foods to avoid

Some foods are oviously made from wheatflour, but many others such as bedtime drinks, baked beans, white pepper, sandwich spreads, salad dressings, instant coffee, pie fillings, mustard and stock cubes may also contain it. One way of checking is to look at the list of ingredients. In addition to the word wheat any of the following items may indicate the presence of gluten.

Barley	Edible starch	Oatmeal	Rye
Bran	Food starch	Pearl barley	Starch
Cornflour	Flour	Rolled oats	thickening
Cornstarch	Oats	Rusk	

Index

African millet bread, 17
almond: almond cake, 123
   almond pastry, 81–2
   Bakewell tart, 90
   crunchy breakfast rice, 23
apple: apple and nut cookies, 110
   apple Charlotte, 101
   corn and apple pancakes, 29
avocado: chicken with avocado, 61
   guacamole sauce, 63

Baisan flour, 3
baked fruit pudding, 100
Bakewell tart, 90
baking powder, 129
barley, gluten content, 1
basic meat gravy, 77
basic white sauce, 78
batters, 74–6
   corn fritters, 76
   fried onion rings, 76
   light batter for tempura fish and
     vegetables, 74
   vegetable pakoras, 75
bean flour, 3
beef: spicy stuffed tacos, 58
biscuits, 129
   apple and nut cookies, 110
   cheese straws, 59
   ginger millet flapjack, 113
   lemon biscuits, 109
   melting moments, 116
   peanut fingers, 111
black eye beans: pulse and pepper
   soup, 38
blue cheese tartlets, 84
bran, 129
Brazil nuts: breakfast yogurt, 24
bread, 5–19

African millet bread, 17
buckwheat loaf, 9
carrot peanut bread, 10
corn and rice bread, 13
corn muffins, 12
cornbread, 12
crusty bread, 8
eggy bread, 31
peanut butter cornbread, 11
Serbian cornmeal bread, 14
spoon bread, 15
white bread, 7
bread and butter pudding, 97
breakfast, 20–31
breakfast yogurt, 24
buckwheat, 2, 3
buckwheat flour, 3
   buckwheat loaf, 9
   buckwheat pancakes stuffed with
     spiced potatoes, 64
buckwheat noodles, 3, 52
buns, rice and raisin, 118

cakes: almond cake, 123
   carob date fingers, 112
   coconut mountains, 111
   cream and jam sponge sandwich,
     120
   date and cherry crispy fingers, 108
   fruit cake, 125
   gingerbread, 117
   lemon curd cake, 121
   lemon rice cake, 124
   potato fruit cake, 126
   refrigerator cake, 127
   rice and nut clusters, 115
   sweet potato cake, 122
   syrup crispies, 114
canapés and snacks, see snacks

carob, 129
  carob date fingers, 112
  'chocolate' cherry pots, 104
  'chocolate' steamed pudding, 96
  creamed carob whip, 106
  date and cherry crispy fingers, 108
  refrigerator cake, 127
  rice and nut clusters, 115
Carolina baked chicken, 73
carrots: carrot and potato soup, 37
  carrot peanut bread, 10
casseroles, 45–51
  chicken à la Moambe, 46
  chicken in red wine, 47
  cod Lyonnaise, 49
  monkfish with vegetable sauce, 48
  rice and vegetable pie, 51
  thickening, 45–6
  vegetable curry with chickpeas, 50
cellophane noodles, see transparent
    noodles
cereals (breakfast), 20
  crunchy breakfast rice, 23
  millet and hazelnut muesli, 22
  mixed cereal muesli, 21
Channa flour, 3
cheese: blue cheese tartlets, 84
  cheese and rice soufflé, 42
  cheese pastry, 81–2
  cheese sauce, 78
  cheese straws, 59
  cheesy baked cod, 71
  cornmeal balls, 57
  deep fried potato balls, 70
  fishcakes in a cheese coating, 72
  millet soup with cheese, 35
  mixed vegetable quiche, 86
  potato-based soufflé, 45
  quick cheese soufflé, 43
  rice and vegetable pie, 51
  scones, 16
  tomato cheese flan, 87
  watercress and rice flan, 89
cheesecake: orange cheesecake flan, 94
cherries, glacé: 'chocolate' cherry pots,
    104
  date and cherry crispy fingers, 108
chestnut stuffing for turkey, 67
chicken: Carolina baked chicken, 73
  chicken à la Moambe, 46

chicken in red wine, 47
chicken soufflé, 44
chicken with avocado, 61
Chinese chicken noodle soup, 33
  sage and onion stuffing for, 68
  stir-fried chicken with transparent
    noodles, 55
chickpea flour, 3
chickpeas, vegetable curry with, 50
Chinese chicken noodle soup, 33
'chocolate' cherry pots, 104
'chocolate' steamed pudding, 96
coatings, 69–76
  Carolina baked chicken, 73
  cheesy baked cod, 71
  for deep-fried fish, 70
  fishcakes in a cheese coating, 72
  lamb chops with a nutty coat, 72
coconut: coconut and pecan flan case,
    92
  coconut mountains, 111
  pineapple ginger flan, 93
  sweet potato pudding, 99
cod: cheesy baked cod, 71
  cod Lyonnaise, 49
coeliac disease, vii
corn, 2, 3
cornbread, 12
  corn and rice bread, 13
  peanut butter cornbread, 11
  Serbian cornmeal bread, 14
cornflakes: Carolina baked chicken, 73
  cheesy baked cod, 71
  coconut and pecan flan case, 92
cornflour, 3
  cheese straws, 59
  corn fritters, 76
  potato rice pastry, 82–3
  scones, 16
cornmeal, 3
  carrot peanut bread, 10
  cheese straws, 59
  corn and apple pancakes, 29
  corn and rice bread, 13
  corn fritters, 76
  corn muffins, 12
  cornbread, 12
  cornmeal balls, 57
  fried polenta squares with poached
    eggs, 26

cornmeal – *cont.*
  peanut butter cornbread, 11
  Serbian cornmeal bread, 14
  spoon bread, 15
courgettes: cream of courgette soup, 39
cream and jam sponge sandwich, 120
cream of courgette soup, 39
creamed carob whip, 106
crispy noodles with sweet and sour pork, 54
crumble, fruit, 98
crunchy breakfast rice, 23
crusty bread, 8
curry: curried egg flan, 88
  vegetable curry with chickpeas, 50

dairy sauces, 80
dates: carob date fingers, 112
  date and cherry crispy fingers, 108
  date and walnut loaf, 119
deep fried potato balls, 70
dermatitis herpetiformis, vii
drop scones, 18

eggs: curried egg flan, 88
  eggy bread, 31
  fried polenta squares with poached eggs, 26
  ham and egg tartlets, 85
  rice and coddled eggs, 30

fennel, rice noodles with prawns and, 53
fish: cheesy baked cod, 71
  coatings for deep-fried fish, 70
  cod Lyonnaise, 49
  fishcakes in a cheese coating, 72
  light batter for tempura fish, 74
  monkfish with vegetable sauce, 48
flans, savoury: curried egg flan, 88
  mixed vegetable quiche, 86
  tomato cheese flan, 87
  watercress and rice flan, 89
flapjack, ginger millet, 113
flour, 1, 5–6, 128, 204
fried onion rings, 76
fried polenta squares with poached eggs, 26
fritters: corn, 76

savoury rice, 65
fruit: baked fruit pudding, 100
  breakfast yogurt, 24
  coconut and pecan flan case, 92
  fruit crumble, 98
  fruit pies, 91
fruit cake, 125
  potato fruit cake, 126

ginger: ginger millet flapjack, 113
  gingerbread, 117
  pear and ginger trifle, 105
  pineapple ginger flan, 93
gluten, 1
gluten-free foods, 2–4
Grain flour, 3
gravy, 77
guacamole sauce, 63

ham: ham and egg tartlets, 85
  rice and coddled eggs, 30
haricot beans: pulse and pepper soup, 38
hazelnuts: hazelnut cake, 123
  millet and hazelnut muesli, 22
herb pastry, 81–2
homemade bread and butter pudding, 97
hot lemon rice soufflé, 102

Indian corn, 2
Indian rice balls, 107

jam: jam pudding, 95
  jam tarts, 91

kidney beans: refried beans, 60

lamb: lamb chops with a nutty coat, 72
  Scotch broth with whole millet, 34
lemon: hot lemon rice soufflé, 102
  lemon biscuits, 109
  lemon curd cake, 121
  lemon pancakes, 103
  lemon rice cake, 124
lentils: pulse and pepper soup, 38
light batter for tempura fish and vegetables, 74

maize flour, 3
maizemeal, 3
  buckwheat loaf, 9

cornmeal balls, 57
potato rice pastry, 82–3
Serbian cornmeal bread, 14
spoon bread, 15
marmalade pudding, 95
melting moments, 116
Mexican tortillas, 6
millet, 2
millet soup with cheese, 35
Scotch broth with whole millet, 34
millet, flaked, 2, 128
African millet bread, 17
breakfast yogurt, 24
cheese and rice soufflé, 42
fishcakes in a cheese coating, 72
ginger millet flapjack, 113
millet and hazelnut muesli, 22
rice and millet porridge, 25
sage and onion stuffing for chicken,
68
mixed cereal muesli, 21
mixed vegetable quiche, 86
monkfish with vegetable sauce, 48
Moong flour, 3
muesli, 20
millet and hazelnut muesli, 22
mixed cereal muesli, 21
muffins, corn, 12
mushrooms, potato pancakes with,
27–8

noodles, 2, 3, 52
Chinese chicken noodle soup, 33
crispy noodles with sweet and sour
pork, 54
rice noodles with prawns and
fennel, 53
stir-fried chicken with transparent
noodles, 55
nuts: apple and nut cookies, 110
date and cherry crispy fingers, 108
deep fried potato balls, 70
lamb chops with a nutty coat, 72
rice and nut clusters, 115

oats, gluten content, 1
One-step (casserole-thickener), 45–6
onion: fried onion rings, 76
onion sauce, 79
sage and onion stuffing for chicken,
68

orange cheesecake flan, 94

pakoras, vegetable, 75
pancakes: buckwheat pancakes
stuffed with spiced potatoes, 64
corn and apple pancakes, 29
lemon pancakes, 103
potato pancakes with mushrooms,
27–8
Scotch, 18
parsley sauce, 79
pasta, 52–5
crispy noodles with sweet and sour
pork, 54
rice noodles with prawns and
fennel, 53
stir-fried chicken with transparent
noodles, 55
pastry, 81–3, 128
cheese, 81–2
potato rice pastry, 82–3
shortcrust, 81–2
peanuts and peanut butter: Carolina
baked chicken, 73
carrot peanut bread, 10
chicken à la Moambe, 46
peanut butter cornbread, 11
peanut fingers, 111
pear and ginger trifle, 105
peas: curried egg flan, 88
rice and coddled eggs, 30
pecan nuts: coconut and pecan flan
case, 92
peppers: pulse and pepper soup, 38
pies, fruit, 91
pineapple ginger flan, 93
polenta: cheese straws, 59
fried polenta squares with poached
eggs, 26
poppadoms, 6
pork: crispy noodles with sweet and
sour pork, 54
porridge, 20
rice and millet porridge, 25
potato: buckwheat pancakes stuffed
with spiced potatoes, 64
carrot and potato soup, 37
cod Lyonnaise, 49
deep fried potato balls, 70
fishcakes in a cheese coating, 72

potato – *cont.*
    potato cakes, 19
    potato fruit cake, 126
    potato pancakes with mushrooms,
        27–8
    potato rice pastry, 82–3
    potato-based soufflé, 45
    refrigerator cake, 127
potato flour, 4
prawns: rice noodles with fennel and,
    53
puddings: apple Charlotte, 101
    baked fruit pudding, 100
    Bakewell tart, 90
    'chocolate' cherry pots, 104
    'chocolate' steamed pudding, 96
    coconut and pecan flan case, 92
    creamed carob whip, 106
    fruit crumble, 98
    homemade bread and butter
        pudding, 97
    hot lemon rice soufflé, 102
    Indian rice balls, 107
    jam or marmalade pudding, 95
    lemon pancakes, 103
    orange cheesecake flan, 94
    pear and ginger trifle, 105
    pineapple ginger flan, 93
    sweet potato pudding, 99
puffed rice cakes, 6
pulse and pepper soup, 38

quick cheese soufflé, 43

raisins: rice and nut clusters, 115
    rice and raisin buns, 118
    scones, 16
refried beans, 60
refrigerator cake, 127
rice, 2
    chestnut stuffing for turkey, 67
    hot lemon rice soufflé, 102
    Indian rice balls, 107
    rice and coddled eggs, 30
    rice and vegetable pie, 51
    savoury rice fritters, 65
    watercress and rice flan, 89
    watercress soup, 40
rice, flaked, 2, 128
    cheese and rice soufflé, 42

crunchy breakfast rice, 23
fishcakes in a cheese coating, 72
rice and millet porridge, 25
sage and onion stuffing for chicken,
    68
rice, ground, 2
    apple and nut cookies, 110
    lemon rice cake, 124
rice bran, 129
rice cakes: carob date fingers, 112
rice crispies: coatings for deep-fried
        fish, 70
    lamb chops with a nutty coat, 72
    pineapple ginger flan, 93
    rice and nut clusters, 115
    syrup crispies, 114
rice flour, 2
    corn and rice bread, 13
    potato rice pastry, 82–3
    rice and raisin buns, 118
    scones, 16
rice noodles, 2, 52
    crispy noodles with sweet and sour
        pork, 54
    rice noodles with prawns and
        fennel, 53
rye, gluten content, 1

sage and onion stuffing for chicken, 68
sauces, 77–80
    basic meat gravy, 77
    basic white sauce, 78
    cheese, 78
    dairy sauces, 80
    guacamole, 63
    onion, 79
    parsley, 79
    tomato, 62, 80
    tomato- and vegetable-based, 79
savoury rice fritters, 65
scones, 16
    drop scones, 18
Scotch broth with whole millet, 34
Scotch pancakes, 18
Serbian cornmeal bread, 14
shortcrust pastry, 81–2
snacks and canapés, 56–65
    buckwheat pancakes stuffed with
        spiced potatoes, 64
    cheese straws, 59

chicken with avocado, 61
cornmeal balls, 57
refried beans, 60
savoury rice fritters, 65
stuffed tacos, 57–8
vegetable pakoras, 75
soufflés, 41–5
cheese and rice, 42
chicken, 44
hot lemon rice, 102
potato-based, 45
quick cheese, 43
soups, 32–40
carrot and potato, 37
Chinese chicken noodle, 33
cream of courgette, 39
millet soup with cheese, 35
pulse and pepper, 38
Scotch broth with whole millet, 34
thickening, 36
watercress, 40
soy sauce, 52
soya bean flakes: vegetarian stuffing
for vegetables, 69
soya bran, 129
soya flour, 3
spicy minced beef stuffed tacos, 58
split green pea flour, 3
spoon bread, 15
stir-fried chicken with transparent
noodles, 55
stock, 32
stock cubes, 32
stuffed tacos, 57–8
stuffings, 66–9
chestnut, for turkey, 67
sage and onion, for chicken, 68
vegetarian, for vegetables, 69
sweet and sour pork, crispy noodles
with, 54
sweet potato: sweet potato cake, 122
sweet potato pudding, 99
sweetcorn, 2, 3
corn and apple pancakes, 29
corn fritters, 76
syrup crispies, 114

tacos: spicy minced beef stuffed tacos,
58

stuffed, 57–8
tamari sauce, 52
tartlets: blue cheese tartlets, 84
ham and egg tartlets, 85
jam tarts, 91
tarts, sweet: Bakewell tart, 90
coconut and pecan flan case, 92
orange cheesecake flan, 94
pineapple ginger flan, 93
tea bread: date and walnut loaf, 119
tempura fish and vegetables, 74
tomato: monkfish with vegetable
sauce, 48
rice and coddled eggs, 30
tomato cheese flan, 87
tomato sauce, 62, 79, 80
tortillas, 6
transparent noodles, 52
stir-fried chicken with, 55
trifle, pear and ginger, 105
turkey, chestnut stuffing for, 67

Urad dal flour, 3

vegetables: mixed vegetable quiche, 86
monkfish with vegetable sauce, 48
rice and vegetable pie, 51
stir-fried chicken with transparent
noodles, 55
tempura, 74
vegetable-based sauces, 79
vegetable curry with chickpeas, 50
vegetable pakoras, 75
vegetarian stuffing for vegetables, 69

walnuts: date and walnut loaf, 119
watercress: watercress and rice flan,
89
watercress soup, 40
wheat, gluten content, 1
wheatflour, 1
white bread, 7
white sauce, 78
wine: chicken in red wine, 47
monkfish with vegetable sauce, 48

yogurt: breakfast yogurt, 24
vegetable curry with chickpeas, 50